National 5
Modern Studies
Practice Papers for SQA Exams

Frank Cooney

Kenneth Hannah

Contents

Introduction	iii
Revision grid	ix
Practice Paper A	1
Practice Paper B	21
Practice Paper C	43
Answers	63

HODDER GIBSON
AN HACHETTE UK COMPANY

The Publishers would like to thank the following for permission to reproduce copyright material:

Photo credits: p.4 *l* © kurhan – 123rf; *r* © Rob – Fotolia; **p.7** *l* © duckman76 – Fotolia; *r* © szefei – 123rf; **p.37** *l* © Monkey Business via Thinkstock/Getty Images; *r* Cathy Yeulet – 123rf; **p.41** *l* © pictrough – 123rf; *r* © Solaria – Fotolia.

Acknowledgements: Exam rubrics at the start of each practice paper Copyright © Scottish Qualifications Authority; **p.10** Source 2, adapted from Chartered Institute and Personnel Development and other sources; **p.11** Source 3, adapted from Resolution Foundation, an independent research and policy organisation and other sources; **p.17** Source 3, National Election Pool – a consortium of ABC News, Associated Press, CBS News, CNN, Fox News and NBC News; pp.**19–20** United Nations 2015; **p.30** Source 2, The Trussell Trust; **p.31** Source 3, The Trussell Trust; pp.**33–34** Sources 1, 2 and 3, The Scottish Government, Contains public sector information licensed under the Open Government Licence v3.0, http://www.nationalarchives.gov.uk/doc/open-government-licence/version/3/; **p.61** Source 3, CIA World Factbook.

Every effort has been made to trace all copyright holders, but if any have been inadvertently overlooked the Publishers will be pleased to make the necessary arrangements at the first opportunity.

Although every effort has been made to ensure that website addresses are correct at time of going to press, Hodder Gibson cannot be held responsible for the content of any website mentioned in this book. It is sometimes possible to find a relocated web page by typing in the address of the home page for a website in the URL window of your browser.

Hachette UK's policy is to use papers that are natural, renewable and recyclable products and made from wood grown in sustainable forests. The logging and manufacturing processes are expected to conform to the environmental regulations of the country of origin.

Orders: please contact Bookpoint Ltd, 130 Park Drive, Milton Park, Abingdon, Oxon OX14 4SE. Telephone: (44) 01235 827720. Fax: (44) 01235 400454. Lines are open 9.00–5.00, Monday to Saturday, with a 24-hour message answering service. Visit our website at www.hoddereducation.co.uk. Hodder Gibson can be contacted direct on: Tel: 0141 333 4650; Fax: 0141 404 8188; Email: hoddergibson@hodder.co.uk

© Frank Cooney and Kenneth Hannah 2016
First published in 2016 by
Hodder Gibson, an imprint of Hodder Education,
An Hachette UK Company
211 St Vincent Street
Glasgow G2 5QY

Impression number   5 4 3 2 1
Year   2020 2019 2018 2017 2016

Cover photo © Marcel Schauer – Fotolia
Illustrations by Aptara, Inc.
Typeset in DIN Regular, 12/14.4 pts. by Aptara Inc.
Printed and bound by CPI Group (UK) Ltd, Croydon, CR0 4YY

A catalogue record for this title is available from the British Library

ISBN: 978 1 4718 8600 3

Introduction

National 5 Modern Studies

Study Skills – what you need to know to pass exams

So you know how to revise and study? Do you use the time wisely and productively or do you find that you cannot concentrate and find excuses to do something else? Below are some common-sense tips to prepare you for the exam.

Start revision in good time and do not leave it to the last moment. Make a revision timetable that sets out a balanced PLAN of study and YOU time.

So, good! You have started early. This gives you time to organise the **first stage** of revision. You should use the following: an up-to-date textbook, class notes/handouts and PowerPoints. Use or find a copy of the course outlines of the topics you will be asked about in your exam. You should make sure that there are no gaps in your knowledge and skills.

Make sure you know what to expect in the exam by being able to answer the following:

- How is the exam paper structured?
- Have any changes been made to the course? (The answer is yes for Modern Studies!)
- What type of questions will be asked and how much time should you devote to each question?
- Which topics are your strongest and which are your weakest?

You are now ready to begin the **second stage**. You should make short summary notes from your textbook or course materials for each of your three topics. You may type them out or use different coloured pens to write them out. Remember to use mind maps and other visual techniques as these are excellent memory aids. This will be time consuming but will be worth it as these notes will be the only ones you will use for your future knowledge revision. You should also practise skills-based questions.

You are now ready for the **third stage** which will take place close to your exam. Research has shown that you feel more positive and retain information better if you are active. Music stimulates the brain and provides a good feeling. So while you are listening to your favourite songs, you could walk up and down the room memorising and reviewing key aspects of the course. **Try it, it works!** Sitting down and gazing at notes will lead to day-dreaming and your mind will wander.

> 'The thing that matters most must never be at the mercy of the things that matter the least.'
>
> **19th-century German writer**

Personal checklist/action plan

- Get your materials organised.
- Always know what you are trying to learn.
- Get rid of distractions.
- Maintain focus.
- Think about it.
- Revise from the beginning.
- Take notes.
- Practice, Practice, Practice!

Congratulations! You have reached the stage where you can answer knowledge questions with confidence and know exactly what is required to gain high marks in your skills questions. You may wish to time yourself to make sure that you can answer questions in the time allotted. This will improve time management and ensure that you will avoid having to rush your questions or, even worse, miss out some questions in the exam.

The Added Value unit for National 5 is an externally marked assessment. This consists of two parts:

- National 5 question paper – 60 marks allocated = 75% of marks
- National 5 assignment – 20 marks allocated = 25% of marks

Total marks available = 80 marks

To gain the course award, all units and course assessments must be passed. The marks you achieve in the question paper and assignment are added together and an overall mark will indicate a pass or fail. From this, your course award will then be graded.

The Modern Studies assignment

Before your exam in May, you will carry out the 'assignment' as part of your National 5 course assessment. Your teacher will probably plan to complete this during the spring term before you sit the exam.

The assignment is your personal research on a Modern Studies topic or issue of your own choice. The information collected should display knowledge and understanding of the topic or issue chosen and should include at least two methods of collecting information, with comment on the effectiveness of the methods used.

Best practice is to choose a hypothesis which is simply a statement that your personal research will try to prove or disprove.

A good example would be: *The voting age in all UK elections should be reduced to 16.*

You may choose a hypothesis or issue from any of the three course units or you may choose a topic that integrates two units of the course, for example: *Health inequalities in Scotland and the USA.*

Some possible titles could include:

- *Poverty is the main cause of health inequalities in Scotland.*
- *Free prescriptions should be given to all groups in England.*
- *The 'not proven' verdict does not deliver justice.*
- *The Educational Maintenance Allowance should be given to all 16+ school students.*

- *The abuse of gun ownership is a major problem in the USA but not in Scotland.*
- *The UK should accept all Syrian refugees who wish to come to our country.*

You will write up the results of your research under controlled assessment conditions on an official SQA double-page pro forma assignment sheet (see below). You will be given one hour to do this.

The assignment is very important as it is worth a total of 20 marks (25% of your overall mark). Of these, 14 marks are for skills and 6 marks are for knowledge and understanding.

You are allowed to bring two single-sided sheets of A4 paper (containing your notes) into the room to refer to during the write-up.

Remember

You will not receive marks for writing out your hypothesis and aims. However, you can write these on your information sheet. This will guide you through your written response.

Pro forma assignment sheet

The pro forma assignment sheet consists of three sections for you to fill in, with marks allocated to each. Below is an outline of the sections.

1 Evaluating research methods (10 marks)

You are expected to evaluate the strengths and weaknesses of the two research methods you have used. You should explain why each method is relevant and highlight its strengths and/or weaknesses. You should make reference to the information which you will take into the assignment. Your A4 information sheet should include evidence of primary and/or secondary research and may include, for example, survey results, interview findings, notes from a textbook, newspapers or websites.

2 Research findings: Presenting your findings clearly (6 marks)

You will have a full page to detail and explain the evidence you have gathered. You may wish to write more and you may request extra sheets. The evidence should be balanced and factually correct and you should consider various viewpoints. You should make reference to your A4 information sheet (the notes you bring into the assignment write-up) in your presentation of your findings.

3 Research conclusion (4 marks)

Your conclusion should be based on the quality of the research evidence you have presented and should link back to your original hypothesis and aims. Try to avoid just repeating findings already given. At this stage you can indicate what your final thoughts on your issue are.

Planning your research

In order to carry out a successful piece of personal research you need to plan it effectively. You will need to keep all evidence of your planning so that your work can be accurately marked.

You may wish to consider the following questions about your primary and secondary sources:

- What useful information have I got from this source to help me research my issue?
- How reliable is the information gathered from the source?
- Could the source contain bias or exaggeration?

Good practice

In your research methods section:

- Give as many advantages and disadvantages as possible BUT keep it personal to your research.
- Suggest for each method used what you would do differently if you carried out this research again.

In your research findings section:

- Make reference to your A4 information sheet. However, you won't receive any marks for copying – so less is best in the information sheet.
- Lay out your answer addressing each AIM.
- Add relevant knowledge and understanding from memory and not from your sheet to achieve 6/6 marks.

In your conclusion section:

- Frame your answer aim by aim, with a relevant conclusion for each.
- Then come to an overall conclusion regarding the hypothesis.

Bad practice

Examples of bad practice include:

- Poor title/hypothesis.
- COPYING in detail from the information sheet.
- General analysis of research methods.
- Research findings that are vague and not relevant to the assignment's aims.
- A short, one paragraph conclusion – this will not gain 4 marks.

The exam

The exam is split into three sections:

- Democracy in Scotland and the United Kingdom
- Social Issues in the United Kingdom
- International Issues

You will usually have studied one topic from each of the three sections above and the questions you will answer in your exam will be on these topics (see table below).

Section	Choice one	Choice two
1 Democracy in Scotland and the United Kingdom	A Democracy in Scotland	**OR** B Democracy in the United Kingdom
2 Social Issues in the United Kingdom	C Social Inequality	**OR** D Crime and the Law
3 International Issues	E World Powers	**OR** F World Issues

The question paper

You will have one hour and 30 minutes to complete the question paper, with a total of 60 marks allocated. There are 26 marks available for skills-based questions and 34 for knowledge and understanding, with 20 marks in total for each of the three exam sections outlined in the table on page vi.

As stated, the paper will be divided into three sections, one per unit, each worth 20 marks. Each section will have three questions. The three questions will be as follows:

- **Describe** (worth either 4, 6 or 8 marks)
  For example:
  Describe, in detail, two ways that an MSP can represent their constituents in the Scottish Parliament.
- **Explain** (worth either 4, 6 or 8 marks)
  For example:
  Explain, in detail, two reasons why some groups in society are more likely to suffer social inequality than others.
- **Source based** (worth either 8 or 10 marks)
  For example:
  Using Sources 1, 2 and 3, what conclusions can be drawn about ...?

The knowledge and skills questions for International Issues will not refer to a particular country or issue. You will be expected to base your 'describe' and 'explain' answers around your knowledge and understanding of the world power or world issue you have studied.

The knowledge and understanding questions

In the exam paper more marks are awarded for knowledge and understanding than skills so it is crucial that you have a sound grasp of content.

Tips for success	Things to avoid
Only answer the exact question that is set.	Don't *turn the question* into something it is not – you won't receive any marks for details or examples that are not relevant.
Use recent examples to illustrate your understanding.	Dated examples should be avoided.
Develop the points you make with detail.	Don't just write a list of facts.
Be aware of the different needs of the **describe** and **explain** questions.	Don't confuse the different types of question.
Use the number of marks allocated to each question as a guide to how much to write.	Don't waste time on the shorter mark questions – you may run out of time on the questions worth the most marks.

The source-based questions

There are three types of source-based skills questions which can appear in any of the three sections of the exam.

Type of source-based question	How to answer this type of question
Use sources of information to identify and explain selective use of facts.	You should: ■ state whether the evidence being used is showing selectivity or not ■ state whether the evidence is supporting or opposing the view.
Use sources of information to make and justify a decision.	You should: ■ justify your decision ■ explain why you have rejected the other option.
Use sources of information to draw and support conclusions.	You should use the headings to draw an overall conclusion which may be given at the beginning or end of the explanation.

Tips for success	Things to avoid
Only use the sources provided.	Don't state your own knowledge or opinions on the topic.
Use **all** the sources provided and link evidence from different sources to give a detailed argument.	Don't just rely on one piece of evidence from a source to provide argument.
Interpret any statistical evidence to show how it links to the question being asked.	Don't just repeat the statistics without interpreting and explaining them.

GOOD LUCK IN YOUR EXAM!

Revision grid

	Practice Paper A		Practice Paper B		Practice Paper C	
	Describe	Explain	Describe	Explain	Describe	Explain
Unit 1 – Democracy in Scotland and the United Kingdom						
Local councils						
How MPs/MSPs represent constituents in parliament			X			
Participation		X			X	X
Election campaigns						
Political institutions Scotland/ UK First Minister/Prime Minister	X					
Voting systems				X		
Unit 2 – Social Issues in the United Kingdom: Social Inequality and Crime and the Law						
Impact of poverty on children	X					
Reasons for social inequalities				X		
Reasons for health inequalities		X				
Groups that tackle social inequality			X			X
Evidence of social inequality					X	
Different types of crime	X				X	
Types of criminal sentences			X			
Alternatives to prison (reasons)		X				
Impact of crimes				X		
Causes of crime						X
Unit 3 – International Issues: World Powers and World Issues						
Political issues – rights and responsibilities	X					
Political issues – participation			X			
Social/Economic inequalities		X		X	X	
Global influence						X
Causes of an international issue	X					
Consequences/Impact of issue			X		X	
Attempts at resolution		X		X		X

Skills questions revision grid

	Democracy in Scotland and the United Kingdom	Social issues in the United Kingdom	International Issues
Paper A	Options	Selectivity	Conclusions
Paper B	Selectivity	Conclusions	Options
Paper C	Conclusions	Options	Selectivity

National 5 Modern Studies

HODDER
GIBSON
LEARN MORE

A

Duration: 1 hour and 30 minutes

Total marks: 60

SECTION 1 – DEMOCRACY IN SCOTLAND AND THE UNITED KINGDOM – 20 marks

Attempt ONE part, EITHER

Part A Democracy in Scotland   Pages 3–5

OR

Part B Democracy in the United Kingdom   Pages 6–8

SECTION 2 – SOCIAL ISSUES IN THE UNITED KINGDOM – 20 marks

Attempt ONE part, EITHER

Part C Social Inequality   Pages 9–11

OR

Part D Crime and the Law   Pages 12–14

SECTION 3 – INTERNATIONAL ISSUES – 20 marks

Attempt ONE part, EITHER

Part E World Powers   Pages 15–17

OR

Part F World Issues   Pages 18–20

Before attempting the questions you must check that your answer booklet is for the same subject and level as this question paper.

Read the questions carefully.

On the answer booklet, you must clearly identify the question number you are attempting.

Use **blue** or **black** ink.

Before leaving the examination room you must give your answer booklet to the Invigilator. If you do not, you may lose all the marks for this paper.

Section 1

SECTION 1 – DEMOCRACY IN SCOTLAND AND THE UNITED KINGDOM – 20 marks

Attempt ONE part, EITHER

Part A Democracy in Scotland   Pages 3–5

OR

Part B Democracy in the United Kingdom   Pages 6–8

Part A – Democracy in Scotland

MARKS

In your answers to Questions 1 and 2 you should give recent examples from Scotland.

Question 1

| The First Minister has important powers in the Scottish Government. |

Describe, **in detail**, **two** important powers of the First Minister in the Scottish Government.

4

Question 2

| Some people in Scotland choose not to vote in elections. |

Explain, **in detail**, **two** reasons why some people in Scotland choose not to vote in elections.

6

Part A (continued)

Question 3

Study Sources 1, 2 and 3 and then answer the question which follows.

You have been asked to recommend who should be your party's candidate in the local council elections in Linburn.

Option 1
Candidate Lucas Watt

Option 2
Candidate Sophie Willis

SOURCE 1 Candidates' statements

Lucas Watt: secondary school teacher, age 44

I support the housing development as in the long run it will provide new facilities for Linburn and will bring in more council tax. This development will provide lots of jobs for the area and should be supported. The creation of a new industrial estate will provide employment opportunities for all.

With severe cuts to local authorities' budgets continuing to be made, we must try to increase our revenue. As such, I support an increase in council tax to protect local services. It has remained frozen for many years.

We have a low crime rate and we cannot justify the reopening of the police station. Police Scotland has to make severe cuts to its budget. We should set up Neighbourhood Watch networks to protect our community.

Many parents are concerned about the future education of their children. The influx of young families to the area could lead to the local primary school having too many pupils and having to turn pupils away. So I support the immediate building of a second primary school and, within six years, an expansion to our secondary school.

Sophie Willis: health worker, age 46

I am against any increase in the council tax as it will hit hard on those in work and on most of our elderly. Our residents face severe pressure on family budgets and the last thing we need is an increase in the council tax.

Our most urgent priority is health provision rather than education. Many of our elderly residents are concerned that the local health centre will soon not be able to meet their health needs. As such I support the immediate building of a second health centre. Our schools can easily cope with the increase in demand and so are not a priority.

I support only a limited housing programme so that we can monitor its effects on Linburn. We already have major parking problems and traffic jams at peak times which create frustration and accidents. I support an improvement in our transport links to manage the increased volume of traffic.

Crime is a major concern in the area and this is reflected in the findings of our Community Council. I will fight for the restoration of our police station. Our elderly population need better protection – they do not feel safe even during the day.

Part A Question 3 (continued)

SOURCE 2

Linburn is a council area in the West of Scotland with a population of about 6,000. It is an established community with over 80 per cent of its residents owning their own homes. Some are concerned that council tax might be raised; others would accept an increase if it means no cuts to education and community health budgets. A new massive private housing development is being built in Linburn which will eventually double the population.

The local secondary school has a very good reputation and standards are high. However, residents are concerned that the present health and educational services will not be able to cope with the increase in population. There are plans to eventually provide a new primary school, community centre and leisure centre. An industrial site is already being built to attract small firms to the area which will improve the local economy.

Linburn is only five miles from the nearest town which has one of the highest crime rates in the country. Many Linburn residents are concerned about the growing crime rate, especially the elderly. Frank Clark, Chair of the Community Council stated, 'More and more residents are contacting me about attempted and actual house break-ins, we need a stronger police presence'.

Profile of Linburn – key statistics (%)

	Linburn	Scotland
Number of pensioners	13	10
Home ownership	82	67
Unemployed and seeking work	5	7
School leavers – 3 or more Highers	40	30
Experiencing long-term poor health	20	18

SOURCE 3

Survey of public opinion in Linburn

	Strongly agree (%)	Agree (%)	Disagree (%)	Strongly disagree (%)
Crime is a growing problem in Linburn	21	28	30	21
Council taxes need to be increased	20	25	35	20
The housing development is good for Linburn	16	38	32	14
The priority for Linburn is a second health centre and a new primary school	18	40	32	10

You must decide which option to recommend, **either** Lucas Watt (Option 1) **or** Sophie Willis (Option 2).

MARKS

(i) Using Sources 1, 2 and 3, **which option would you choose**?

(ii) Give reasons to **support** your choice.

(iii) Explain why you did not choose the other option.

Your answer must be based on all **three** sources.

10

[NOW GO TO SECTION 2 ON PAGE 9]

Part B – Democracy in the United Kingdom

In your answers to Questions 4 and 5 you should give recent examples from the United Kingdom.

Question 4

The Prime Minister has important powers in the UK Government.

Describe, **in detail**, **two** important powers of the Prime Minister in the UK Government.

4

Question 5

Some people in the UK choose not to vote in elections.

Explain, **in detail**, **two** reasons why some people in the UK choose not to vote in elections.

6

Part B (continued)

Question 6

Study Sources 1, 2 and 3 and then answer the question which follows.

The Scottish parliamentary constituency of Inverbank held a by-election in April 2016 to elect a new MP. You must decide who you would have chosen to be the party's candidate.

Option 1	Option 2
Candidate Gemma Healy	Candidate Lewis Elliot

SOURCE 1 Candidates' statements

Gemma Healy: social worker, age 28

Women are under-represented across all senior management posts in the UK. We need to send out a political message that this must end. The best way to do this is for me to become our MP and a role model for all women.

I believe we should leave the EU by voting 'No' in the forthcoming referendum on EU membership. We pay too much into the EU and it is not working. EU countries which are using the euro, such as Greece, are in a mess.

I am totally against the UK having nuclear weapons and as such I am against the renewal of the Trident nuclear programme at the Faslane base on the Clyde. The billions of pounds being spent on it should be spent on education and health.

I am against the welfare cuts to public services being imposed by the UK Government. They will hit those on a low income the most. We must protect our families and prevent an increase in child poverty. However, I do not support pensioners getting a winter fuel allowance of £200 per household.

Lewis Elliot: local councillor, age 48

I support the renewal of the Trident nuclear weapons programme at the Faslane base on the river Clyde as it will safeguard the jobs of those who work there. If the new Trident submarines are not built, unemployment will increase.

My priority is to fight against the savage welfare cuts being imposed on the most vulnerable and needy in our community. We need to protect our families and the elderly and I support the payment of the winter fuel allowance.

We need to attract new jobs to the area to alleviate the high unemployment figures. Too many people are not in work and rely on state benefits to get by. If elected, I will work with Scottish Enterprise to achieve this.

I believe we should stay in the EU. I will vote 'Yes' to remain in the EU in the forthcoming referendum on EU membership. We are only a small island and we need the political and economic strength of the EU. We need to work together to resolve the migrant crisis.

Part B Question 6 (continued)

SOURCE 2

Inverbank is a constituency for the UK parliament in central Scotland. Inverbank is a former industrial town with a declining and ageing population. It has a proud industrial heritage but the main employer now is a large call centre. The constituency is high in the deprivation index and the number of people using foodbanks has doubled in the last four years. Income deprivation is high. Average life expectancy in Inverbank is only 68 compared to the UK average of 80.

The party supports fairer gender representation in parliament and is in favour of positive discrimination. However, local party members believe that the choice of candidate should be based on experience and ability, and not just gender.

The number of skilled jobs in the area is declining. One important employer is the Ministry of Defence at the Trident Faslane base on the Clyde. A significant number of skilled and unskilled workers travel there every day. Michelle Daly, Chair of the Community Council, stated, 'Some constituents are very concerned about any decision not to renew Trident, as many will lose their jobs if the base is closed'.

Profile of Inverbank – key statistics (%)

	Inverbank	Scotland
Number of pensioners	13	10
Claiming benefits	20	15
School leavers with no qualifications	13	9
Experiencing long-term poor health	21	18
Visit a food bank on a regular basis	9	6

SOURCE 3

Survey of public opinion in Inverbank (%)

	The Trident nuclear deterrent based at Faslane should be closed	The UK parliament needs more female MPs	Welfare cuts impact most on the poor	The UK should remain in the EU
Strongly agree	20	20	24	16
Agree	32	38	48	40
Disagree	40	25	20	30
Strongly disagree	8	17	8	14

You must decide which option to recommend, **either** Gemma Healy (Option 1) **or** Lewis Elliot (Option 2).

MARKS

(i) Using Sources 1, 2 and 3, **which option would you choose**?

(ii) Give reasons to **support** your choice.

(iii) **Explain** why you did not choose the other option.

Your answer must be based on all **three** sources.

10

[NOW GO TO SECTION 2 ON PAGE 9]

SECTION 2 – SOCIAL ISSUES IN THE UNITED KINGDOM – 20 marks

Attempt ONE part, EITHER

Part C Social Inequality   Pages 9–11

OR

Part D Crime and the Law   Pages 12–14

Part C – Social Inequality

MARKS

In your answers to Questions 7 and 8 you should give recent examples from the United Kingdom.

Question 7

Living in poverty can have a severe impact on children.

Describe, **in detail**, **two** ways in which poverty can have a severe impact on children.

4

Question 8

Health inequalities still exist in the UK.

Explain, **in detail**, the reasons why health inequalities still exist in the UK.

You should give a **maximum** of **three** reasons in your answer.

8

Part C (continued)

Question 9

Study Sources 1, 2 and 3 and then answer the question which follows.

SOURCE 1

Facts and viewpoints about zero-hours contracts

A zero-hours contract is a form of employment contract under which an employer does not have to state how many hours the employee will work per week. This means employees work only when they are needed by their employer. They will only be paid for the hours they work. So on one particular week the employee may only work 15 hours but 30 hours the following week.

This type of work contract is being used increasingly by UK employers. In 2015 the figure stood at an estimated 900,000 compared to 650,000 in 2013.

Well-known companies such as McDonald's and Sports Direct use these contracts as do the NHS and charities. Zero-hours contracts are higher among young people than other age groups with 37 per cent of those employed on such contracts aged between 16 and 24.

Viewpoint of Michelle Kelly: retired clerical assistant

Although retired, I am working part time on a zero-hours contract which gives me flexibility and keeps me active. I can spend time with my grandchildren and the income I receive allows me to have a better standard of living. I work alongside some university students who can combine their studies with some work and income. My employer is happy with this arrangement, and I am in control of my work–life balance. So I am happy to have a zero-hours contract.

Viewpoint of Sam Gunn: hotel worker

I am on a zero-hours contract and I feel I am being exploited by my employer. My contract effectively stops me from taking a second job even if I am down for only 10 hours for the coming week as my contract states that I must be available at all times. These contracts mean employers avoid redundancy pay and pension contributions. I would prefer guaranteed weekly hours so that I can plan my finances. Some months I have to use foodbanks and take out payday loans with very high interest rates.

SOURCE 2

Survey findings of employment satisfaction – zero-hour and non zero-hour workers (2014)

	Zero-hours contract	Non zero-hours contract
Satisfied with job	50%	57%
Work–life balance	65%	58%
Prefer more hours	45%	10%

Part C Question 9 (continued)

SOURCE 3

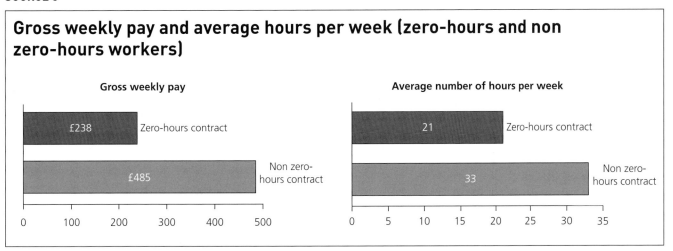

Gross weekly pay and average hours per week (zero-hours and non zero-hours workers)

Using Sources 1, 2 and 3, explain why the view of **Ryan Willis is selective in the use of facts**.

> Zero-hours contract workers are exploited by their employers.
>
> View of Ryan Willis

MARKS

In your answer you must:

- give evidence from the sources that support Ryan Willis' view

  and

- give evidence from the sources that oppose Ryan Willis' view.

Your answer must be based on all **three** sources.

8

[NOW GO TO SECTION 3 ON PAGE 15]

Part D – Crime and the Law

In your answers to Questions 10 and 11 you should give recent examples from the United Kingdom.

Question 10

> Some young people are found guilty of crimes.

Describe, **in detail**, **two** types of crime which young people often commit.

4

Question 11

> Scottish courts are now more willing to use alternative punishments to prison when sentencing offenders.

Explain, **in detail,** why Scottish courts are now more willing to use alternative punishments to prison when sentencing offenders.

You should give a **maximum** of **three** reasons in your answer.

8

Part D (continued)

Question 12

Study Sources 1, 2 and 3 and then answer the question which follows.

SOURCE 1

Facts and viewpoints on the use of taser guns

A taser or stun gun uses compressed air to fire two darts that trail electric cables back to the handset. When the dart strikes, a five second 50,000-volt charge is released that causes the suspect's muscles to contract uncontrollably.

Police officers who are issued with taser guns go on a three-day training course. All of these officers are properly trained. Any use of a taser must be recorded and its use justified.

An officer can point a taser gun at an individual which creates a red dot. This usually leads to the individual ending their aggressive behaviour.

A police official stated: 'I know it is controversial, but tasers are an effective and non-lethal way of stopping a criminal in their tracks'. However, innocent people can be tasered.

The youngest person a taser gun was used on in the UK was a 14-year-old boy. In the USA over 300 people have died after being tasered.

In 2014, 10,400 incidents were logged of police having a taser gun. However, they were only used in 20 per cent of the incidents. The availability of taser guns may damage the trust that exists between the police and UK citizens.

SOURCE 2

The debate over the use of tasers

I was stabbed with a ten-inch butcher's knife while on duty and required extensive surgery. I was off work for six months and I still have nightmares about what happened. I could easily have died and left my three children without a father. If I had a taser gun, I could have protected myself and the public. I could easily have disarmed the criminal. Violent crime is rising and the life of a police officer is becoming more dangerous.

Viewpoint of a London Police Officer

The increase in the use of taser guns is of major concern. Taser guns are a danger to the public and evidence from the USA supports this claim. Taser guns are widely used in the USA. In recent years several men have died in England after being tasered. Mistakes can also be made by the police, for example, in 2012 a police officer tasered a blind man. The police officer thought that his white cane was a Samurai sword!

Viewpoint of a human rights supporter

Part D Question 12 (continued)

SOURCE 3

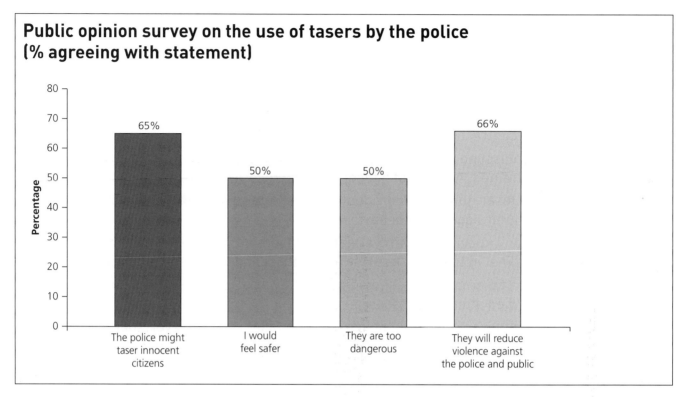

Public opinion survey on the use of tasers by the police (% agreeing with statement)

Using Sources 1, 2 and 3, explain why the view of **Catherine Daly is selective in the use of facts**.

> The use of taser guns is a danger to all.
>
> View of Catherine Daly

MARKS

In your answer you must:

- give evidence from the sources that support Catherine Daly's view

and

- give evidence from the sources that oppose Catherine Daly's view.

Your answer must be based on all **three** sources.

8

[NOW GO TO SECTION 3 ON PAGE 15]

Part E – World Powers

MARKS

In your answers to Questions 13 and 14 you should give recent examples from a world power you have studied.

Question 13

> Citizens enjoy a range of rights and responsibilities.

Describe, **in detail**, the rights and responsibilities of citizens from a world power you have studied.

In your answer you **must** state the world power you have studied.   6

Question 14

> Social and economic inequalities exist in all world powers.

Explain, **in detail**, **two** reasons why social and economic inequalities exist in a world power you have studied.

In your answer you **must** state the world power you have studied.   6

Part E (continued)

Question 15

Study Sources 1, 2 and 3 and then answer the question which follows.

SOURCE 1

USA presidential elections

Elections for President are held every four years. President Obama, the Democratic Party candidate, won his first presidential election in 2008 and was re-elected in 2012.

The President of the USA is not chosen directly by the US people. The Electoral College elects the President. Each state receives a set number of Electoral College votes depending on its population size. For example, Florida with a large population receives 29 Electoral College votes compared to the 3 received by Vermont which has a small population.

There are 538 Electoral College votes in total. Citizens in each state vote for their respective presidential candidates. The candidate with the most votes in say, Florida, wins all of the Electoral College votes of that state.

In 2008, the Democratic candidate Barack Obama made history by becoming the first African-American President of the USA. Obama secured victory with the highest ever recorded popular votes (the total number of votes received across the 50 states). Obama received over 66 million popular votes and he received 365 votes in the Electoral College.

In the 2012 Presidential election, Obama was re-elected President. He received over 65 million votes compared to the Republican candidate, Mick Romney, who won 61 million votes. In the Electoral College, Obama won 332 votes compared to the Republican candidate who won 206.

In the 2012 election, the young, poorer groups and those from an ethnic minority background tended to support Obama, while older and white voters tended to favour the Republican candidate.

SOURCE 2

US presidential election results 2012 and 2008

Party and candidate	Popular Vote 2012	Popular Vote 2008
Democrats: Obama	52.9%	51.0%
Republican: Romney	45.6%	47.1%

Party and candidate	Electoral College 2012	Electoral College 2008
Democrats: Obama	61.7%	67.8%
Republican: Romney	38.3%	32.2%

Part E Question 15 (continued)

SOURCE 3

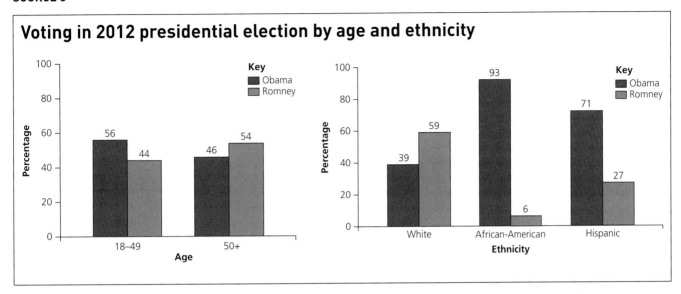

Voting in 2012 presidential election by age and ethnicity

MARKS

Using Sources 1, 2 and 3, what **conclusions** can be drawn about the 2012 USA presidential election?

You should reach a conclusion about **each** of the following:

- the Electoral College results of 2012 compared to 2008
- the popular vote results of 2012 compared to 2008
- the link between age and ethnicity and voting behaviour in the 2012 election.

Your conclusions **must** be supported by evidence from the sources. You should link information within and between the sources in support of your conclusions.

Your answer must be based on all **three** sources.

8

Part F – World Issues

In your answers to Questions 16 and 17 you should give recent examples from a world issue you have studied.

Question 16

International issues are caused by many factors.

Describe, **in detail**, **two** causes of an international issue or conflict you have studied.

6

Question 17

International organisations work hard to resolve international issues and conflicts.

Select an international organisation you have studied.

Explain, **in detail**, **two** reasons why it has succeeded **or** failed in resolving an international issue or conflict.

6

Part F (continued)

Question 18

Study Sources 1, 2 and 3 and then answer the question which follows.

SOURCE 1

Progress in development and aid

In September 2015, the United Nations held a special conference to unveil the Sustainable Development Goals (SDGs) that will shape aid and development for the next 15 years. The conference was attended by the largest gathering ever of world leaders and donors such as Bill Gates. The new SDGs replace the previous Millennium Development Goals (MDGs) which have mostly been achieved largely because of progress in China and India.

However, one area that has been disappointing is the failure of the wealthiest countries to honour their promise to increase their spending on development aid. Of the leading nations only the United Kingdom has reached the agreed goal of spending 0.7 per cent of their Gross Domestic Income (GDI). The USA would argue that they spend $33 billion a year on foreign aid which is the highest for any country (the UK spends $19 million). However, given the massive wealth of the USA this is an insignificant amount of their GDP.

One area of progress is in the determination of the international community, with support from wealthy donors such as Bill Gates, to tackle the killer diseases of malaria and HIV/AIDS. Africa has the highest number of those infected by these diseases. Of the 34 million world citizens who have AIDS, a staggering 24 million live in Africa.

Malaria is responsible for about 450,000 deaths a year. International campaigns have significantly reduced this figure – in 2000 the number of deaths was double the present figure. Swaziland is moving to becoming the first malaria-free country in sub-Saharan Africa (the area that suffers most from the disease).

SOURCE 2

Average wealth per adult in dollars – by region

Africa	5,080
Asia	31,715
Europe	135,977
South America	22,997
North America	340,340

The global HIV/AIDS epidemic by percentage

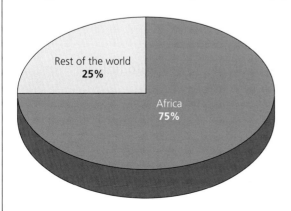

Part F Question 18 (continued)

Foreign aid as a % of GNI (Gross National Income)

United Kingdom	0.70
Germany	0.40
France	0.35
Canada	0.25
Japan	0.19
United States	0.19
Italy	0.16

SOURCE 3

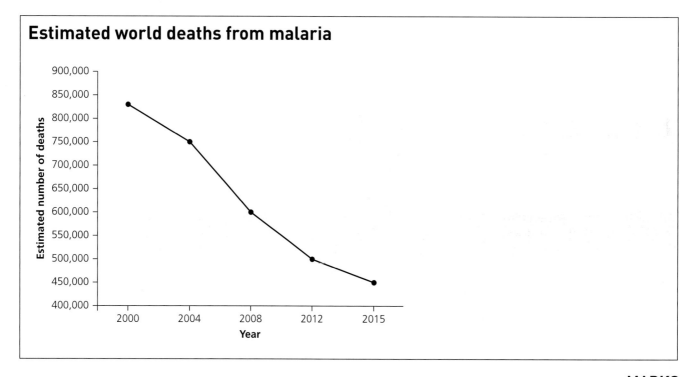

Estimated world deaths from malaria

MARKS

Using Sources 1, 2 and 3, what **conclusions** can be drawn about progress in development and aid?

You should reach a conclusion about each of the following:

- the progress made in reducing deaths from malaria
- the progress among rich countries to achieve the agreed GNI target on development spending
- the link between regional poverty and the existence of killer diseases.

Your conclusions **must** be supported by evidence from the sources. You should link information within and between the sources in support of your conclusions.

Your answer must be based on all **three** sources.

8

[END OF PRACTICE PAPER A]

National 5
Modern Studies

Duration: 1 hour and 30 minutes

Total marks: 60

SECTION 1 – DEMOCRACY IN SCOTLAND AND THE UNITED KINGDOM – 20 marks

Attempt ONE part, EITHER

Part A Democracy in Scotland   Pages 23–25

OR

Part B Democracy in the United Kingdom   Pages 26–28

SECTION 2 – SOCIAL ISSUES IN THE UNITED KINGDOM – 20 marks

Attempt ONE part, EITHER

Part C Social Inequality   Pages 29–31

OR

Part D Crime and the Law   Pages 32–34

SECTION 3 – INTERNATIONAL ISSUES – 20 marks

Attempt ONE part, EITHER

Part E World Powers   Pages 35–38

OR

Part F World Issues   Pages 39–42

Before attempting the questions you must check that your answer booklet is for the same subject and level as this question paper.

Read the questions carefully.

On the answer booklet, you must clearly identify the question number you are attempting.

Use **blue** or **black** ink.

Before leaving the examination room you must give your answer booklet to the Invigilator. If you do not, you may lose all the marks for this paper.

Section 1

SECTION 1 – DEMOCRACY IN SCOTLAND AND THE UNITED KINGDOM – 20 marks

Attempt ONE part, EITHER

Part A Democracy in Scotland   Pages 23–25

OR

Part B Democracy in the United Kingdom   Pages 26–28

Part A – Democracy in Scotland

MARKS

*In your answers to Questions 1 and 2 you should give recent examples
from Scotland.*

Question 1

> There are many ways that an MSP can represent their constituents in the
> Scottish Parliament.

Describe, **in detail**, **two** ways that an MSP can represent their constituents
in the Scottish Parliament.

4

Question 2

> Some people believe that the voting system used to elect MSPs has many
> strengths.

Explain, **in detail**, why some people believe that the voting system used
to elect MSPs has many strengths.

You should give a **maximum** of **three** reasons in your answer.

8

B

Question 3

Study Sources 1, 2 and 3 and then answer the question which follows.

SOURCE 1

Factfile on Scottish Independence Referendum 2014

The Independence Referendum was held on 18 September 2014. Voters were asked, 'Should Scotland be an independent country?'

The 'Yes' campaign was led by Alex Salmond and Nicola Sturgeon. The 'No' by Jim Murphy and Alistair Darling.

Both campaigns were split along party political lines. The 'No' campaign was supported by Labour, the Conservatives and the Liberal Democrats. The 'Yes' by the SNP and the Green Party. Social media was used extensively by both sides, as was old media in the form of street rallies and empty upturned crates.

Throughout the campaign the main issues were to do with the economic impact if Scotland was to become independent including future oil revenues and what currency would be used if independence occurred.

Over 4 million voters were eligible to vote. On the day, 3.6 million people turned out to vote. Just under 85 per cent of voters who could vote, did.

The result saw the 'No' campaign victorious winning just over 55 per cent of the vote compared to the 'Yes' campaign's total of just under 45 per cent. In terms of actual votes, the 'No' campaign achieved 2 million votes. The 'Yes' campaign totalled 1.6 million.

The counting of the votes was via the 32 Scottish council areas. The 'No' campaign won 28 of these areas compared to only 4 for 'Yes'.

SOURCE 2

Selected campaign views

'No' voter

It was a hard-fought campaign. A very hard battle but our arguments about keeping Scotland part of the UK were strongest and we managed to convince the voters that we were right about being 'better together'. An excellent campaign was led by Jim Murphy saying 'No Thanks' to independence. Our arguments on the costs of independence, what currency we would use and economic uncertainty echoed with voters all over Scotland. The final result? 28 areas voted 'No'. Only 4 voted 'Yes'. You can't argue with that. A clear victory for 'No'.

'Yes' voter

It was a hard-fought campaign. I thought 'Yes' did very well to engage so many younger voters. We ran the 'No' campaign close and at one stage, we were even ahead in the opinion polls. The campaign energised many new voters and the way the 'Yes' campaign engaged with voters on social media shows that there are many positives to take out of this referendum result. It was good that Glasgow, the biggest city in Scotland, voted 'Yes' and shows that our message got across to some, but sadly not enough, voters. However, the 55 per cent 'No' to 45 per cent 'Yes' margin was a lot narrower than many people were predicting a year before the vote.

Part A Question 3 (continued)

SOURCE 3 Selected referendum statistics

How Scotland's four main cities voted

City	Yes	No
Dundee	57%	43%
Glasgow	53.5%	46.5%
Edinburgh	39%	61%
Aberdeen	41%	59%

Voting by age

Age	16–24	25–34	35–44	45–54	54–64	65+
Yes	51%	59%	53%	52%	43%	27%
No	49%	41%	47%	48%	57%	63%

Voting by selected council area

Area	Yes	No
Dumfries	34%	66%
Orkney	33%	67%
North Ayrshire	49%	51%
Inverclyde	49.92%	50.08%
East Renfrewshire	37%	63%
Highland	47%	53%
Shetland	36%	64%
Falkirk	47%	53%
West Dunbartonshire	54%	46%

Using Sources 1, 2 and 3, explain why the view of **Bruce Hart is selective in the use of facts**.

> The Scottish Independence Referendum was a massive disappointment for the 'Yes' campaign.
>
> **View of Bruce Hart**

MARKS

In your answer you must:

- give evidence from the sources that support Bruce Hart's view

and

- give evidence from the sources that oppose Bruce Hart's view.

Your answer must be based on all **three** sources.

8

[NOW GO TO SECTION 2 ON PAGE 29]

Part B – Democracy in the United Kingdom

In your answers to Questions 4 and 5 you should give recent examples from the United Kingdom.

Question 4

> There are many ways that an MP can represent their constituents in Parliament.

Describe, **in detail**, **two** ways that an MP can represent their constituents in Parliament.

4

Question 5

> Some people believe that the voting system used to elect MPs has many strengths.

Explain, **in detail**, why some people believe that the voting system used to elect MPs has many strengths.

8

You should give a **maximum** of **three** reasons in your answer.

Part B (continued)

Question 6

Study Sources 1, 2 and 3 and then answer the question which follows.

SOURCE 1

Factfile on the UK 2015 General Election

The UK General Election was held on 7 May 2015. The previous government had been a coalition government between the Conservative Party and the Liberal Democrats. Many political commentators and opinion polls had indicated that the result was going to be another coalition government, with Labour likely to be the largest party.

Voting took place across the UK's 650 constituencies with the campaigns being led by the Conservative's David Cameron, Labour's Ed Miliband and the Lib Dems' Nick Clegg. In Scotland, the SNP's campaign was led by their new leader and First Minister, Nicola Sturgeon.

The Conservatives won the election and increased their number of MPs to become the government with a majority of 12 seats. Labour were the second largest party but dropped 26 seats from their 2010 General Election total, despite seeing an increase in their share of the vote.

It was an election notable for a number of things: the promised UKIP breakthrough didn't occur; the Lib Dems were nearly wiped out, losing 49 of their 57 seats and Labour suffered a near similar fate in Scotland where they went from being the largest party in Scotland to having only one MP.

After the election, Nigel Farage (UKIP), Ed Miliband (Labour) and Nick Clegg (Lib Dems), resigned as the leaders of their parties. The lack of leaders in each of these parties led the SNP to claim that it wasn't Labour that was the Official Opposition Party but the SNP.

SOURCE 2

Campaign analysis

I thought Labour's campaign during the 2015 General Election was well run and focused on the key issues of the economy and the welfare state. I think we got our message across on social media very well but it was in the old media such as newspapers that I thought we struggled. Many of the newspapers were against us from the start. They didn't like Ed very much and this made it difficult to get positive messages in the press.

That said, when you look at and break down some of the election statistics, things aren't as bad as they appear. Our share of the vote went up and in specific groups, Labour did well.

Alistair Tucker – Labour's Campaign Manager

2015 was great for David Cameron and the Conservatives. Not only were we rewarded by the voters for five solid years as the senior partner in the Coalition Government, we were also returned as the majority party which means we don't have to rely on any other party.

The best possible outcome for the Conservatives. All our major rivals losing seats. Labour lost a couple of dozen, the Lib Dems nearly 50 and the much promised UKIP challenge never happened. One seat won by UKIP and it wasn't even their leader's, Nigel Farage. It was the most unexpected of outcomes. As for Scotland, Labour's grip on that part of the UK has gone.

Toby Neil – Conservative Blogger

Part B Question 6 (continued)

SOURCE 3 Selected statistics from the 2015 UK General Election

Change in the share of the vote from the 2010 General Election

UKIP	+9.5%
SNP	+3.1%
Green	+2.8%
Labour	+1.5%
Conservative	+0.5%
Liberal Democrat	-15.2%

Voting by age

Party	18–24	25–34	35–44	45–54	55–64	65+
Conservative	27%	33%	35%	36%	37%	47%
Labour	34%	36%	35%	33%	31%	23%

Using Sources 1, 2 and 3, explain why the view of **David Trotter is selective in the use of facts**.

> The 2015 General Election was a massive disappointment for the Labour Party.
>
> **View of David Trotter**

In your answer you must:

- give evidence from the sources that support David Trotter's view

and

- give evidence from the sources that oppose David Trotter's view.

Your answer must be based on all **three** sources.

MARKS

8

[NOW GO TO SECTION 2 ON PAGE 29]

SECTION 2 – SOCIAL ISSUES IN THE UNITED KINGDOM – 20 marks

Attempt ONE part, EITHER

Part C Social Inequality   Pages 29–31

OR

Part D Crime and the Law   Pages 32–34

Part C – Social Inequality

MARKS

In your answers to Questions 7 and 8 you should give recent examples from the United Kingdom.

Question 7

Governments and organisations have tried to tackle social inequality.

Describe, **in detail**, **two** ways that Government has tried to tackle a social inequality that you have studied.

6

Question 8

Some groups in society are more likely to suffer social inequality than others.

Explain, **in detail**, **two** reasons why some groups in society are more likely to suffer social inequality than others.

6

Part C (continued)

Question 9

Study Sources 1, 2 and 3 and then answer the question which follows.

SOURCE 1

The Department for Work and Pensions (DWP) can impose sanctions on claimants who are deemed to have failed to fulfil the conditions they are required to satisfy in order to receive their benefit payment. Sanctions involve benefit claimants losing all or a proportion of their benefit amount for a certain period of time. There has been an increase in the number of benefit sanctions carried out by the DWP. Since 2010 the rate of benefit sanctions has doubled. This has led to many individuals turning to foodbanks for assistance and help.

Foodbanks offer users a mix of services with donations often coming from members of the public. Many football clubs and local councils have organised foodbank collections. Benefits issues such as benefit changes and delays to payments are often the reasons that many individuals are referred to foodbanks. Many foodbanks are staffed by volunteers and are often organised by local churches, mosques or local community groups. The Trussell Trust is the UK's largest provider of foodbanks.

SOURCE 2

Causes of referrals to foodbanks

Benefit delays	29.6%
Low income	22.2%
Benefit changes	13.8%
Debt	7.2%
Homelessness	4.9%
Other	11.6%

Food aid provision across eight locations

Location	Total	Providing food parcels	Providing hot food
Glasgow	35	26	27
Dundee	12	3	9
Inverness	1	1	0
Fort William	1	1	0
Stirling	2	1	1
Falkirk	2	1	1
Kirriemuir	1	1	0
Forfar	1	1	0

Part C Question 9 (continued)

SOURCE 3

Number of people given three days emergency food parcels by Trussell Trust Foodbanks since 2010	
2010–11	61,488
2011–12	128,697
2012–13	146,992
2013–14	913,138
2014–15	1,084,604

MARKS

Using Sources 1, 2 and 3, what **conclusions** can be drawn about foodbanks?

You should reach a conclusion about each of the following:

■ benefits issues and referrals to foodbanks
■ benefit sanctions and the use of foodbanks since 2010
■ foodbanks and the services provided by them.

Your conclusions **must** be supported by evidence from the sources. You should link information within and between the sources in support of your conclusions.

Your answer must be based on all **three** sources.

8

[NOW GO TO SECTION 3 ON PAGE 35]

Part D – Crime and the Law

In your answers to Questions 10 and 11 you should give recent examples from the United Kingdom.

Question 10

> Apart from prison, there are a variety of sentences that courts can use when dealing with offenders.

Describe, **in detail**, **two** sentences other than prison that courts can use when dealing with offenders.

6

Question 11

> Some groups in society are more likely to be victims of crime than others.

Explain, **in detail**, **two** reasons why some groups in society are more likely to be victims of crime than others.

6

Part D (continued)

Question 12

Study Sources 1, 2 and 3 and then answer the question which follows.

SOURCE 1

Crime rates in Scotland

Recorded crime is at its lowest level since 1974. The overall crime rate has fallen. The total number of crimes recorded by the police in 2016 in Scotland was 256,350. This is 5 per cent lower than the previous year's level. Other than a slight increase in 2006–07, crime has been on a downward trend in Scotland since 2005–06, having decreased overall by 39 per cent. This continues a steadily decreasing trend in recorded crime in Scotland over the last 24 years, from a peak in 1991 when crime reached a record high of 572,921. The clear up rate for all crimes has increased on previous years. In 2012–13 it was at 51 per cent but has increased by 1 per cent to 52 per cent.

The overall decrease in recorded crime was reflected in 23 of the 32 local authority areas, with four experiencing an increase and five with very little change from the previous year. Year on year figures can vary across local authorities, however, the long-term trend is broadly the same across Scotland. Since 2005–06, all local authorities are showing a decrease in recorded crime, varying from 27 per cent in East Ayrshire to 61 per cent in Eilean Siar. There were 479 recorded crimes per 10,000 population in 2014–15. There was a significant difference, however, in recorded crime rates between the most and least populated areas of Scotland.

In addition to the information on police recorded crime, crime in Scotland is also measured by the SCJS, a national survey with adults (aged 16 and over) living in private households which asks respondents about their experiences of crime.

SOURCE 2

Individual crime rates

Crimes of violence decreased by 6 per cent from 6,785 to 6,357 between 2013–14 and 2014–15.

Sexual crimes increased by 11 per cent from 8,604 to 9,557 between 2013–14 and 2014–15.

Crimes of dishonesty decreased by 8 per cent from 137,324 to 126,857 between 2013–14 and 2014–15.

Fire-raising, vandalism, etc. decreased by 4 per cent from 54,418 to 52,091 between 2013–14 and 2014–15.

Other crimes decreased by 3 per cent from 63,266 to 61,488 between 2013–14 and 2014–15.

Part D Question 12 (continued)

SOURCE 3 Selected crime statistics

Crime rates and geographical location (total number of recorded crimes per 10,000 of population 2014–15)

Glasgow, City of	796
Edinburgh, City of	723
Aberdeen, City of	608
Dundee, City of	578
East Ayrshire	489
Fife	389
Dumfries and Galloway	330
Scottish Borders	280
Shetland Isles	190
Eilean Siar	163
Orkney Islands	145

Clear up rate for specific crimes

Crime	2012–13	2013–14
Violent crime	79%	82%
Sexual crime	68%	76%
Dishonesty	37%	36%
Fire-raising/vandalism	25%	27%

MARKS

Using Sources 1, 2 and 3, what **conclusions** can be drawn about crime in Scotland?

You should reach a conclusion about each of the following:

- overall clear up rate compared to clear up rate for specific crimes
- crime rates and geographical location
- overall crime rate compared to individual crime rates.

Your conclusion **must** be supported by evidence from the sources. You should link information within and between sources in support of your conclusion.

Your answer must be based on all **three** sources.

8

[NOW GO TO SECTION 3 ON PAGE 35]

SECTION 3 – INTERNATIONAL ISSUES – 20 marks

Attempt ONE part, EITHER

Part E World Powers   Pages 35–38

OR

Part F World Issues   Pages 39–42

Part E – World Powers

MARKS

In your answers to Questions 13 and 14 you should give recent examples from a world power you have studied.

Question 13

> There are many opportunities for people to participate in the political decision making process.

Describe, **in detail**, **two** ways that people can participate in the political decision making process in the world power you have studied.

In your answer you should state the world power you have studied.

4

Question 14

> Some people think that policies introduced to tackle social and economic inequality have had limited success.

Explain, **in detail**, why some people think that policies introduced to tackle social and economic inequality have had limited success in the world power you have studied.

In your answer you should state the world power you have studied.

6

B

Question 15

Study Sources 1, 2 and 3 and then answer the question which follows.

You have to choose which candidate you think would be the best choice as President of G20 country, Pimlico.

Option 1	Option 2
Hilary Kennedy	Ben Curtis

SOURCE 1

Factfile on Pimlico

Pimlico is a democratic nation that is a member of the G20. It is also a member of the United Nations. It has population of 70 million and is considered to be one of the leading economies in the world.

Like many other countries, it has been in recession following the recent global economic crash. This has created rising prices and increased unemployment in the last few years. Some political leaders have tried to use the increased unemployment figures to restrict immigration to Pimlico. Immigration has never been a key election issue in Pimlico. Immigrants are seen as making a positive contribution to the cultural and economic life of Pimlico.

The government has had to introduce some charges for healthcare which has caused a lot of anger and some demonstrations in the streets against the charges, particularly when the government has increased defence spending for the fourth year running. The plan to introduce charging for some types of healthcare remains deeply unpopular.

Pimlico has not been directly involved in the War on Terror in Iraq, Afghanistan or Syria. It has not participated in any aerial bombing or offered armed forces personnel. Unlike other nations, Pimlico hasn't been the target of any terrorist attacks.

Pimlico's main area of employment used to be heavy industry such as coal mining and shipbuilding. Since the decline of these types of industries, Pimlico has built its financial services sector by attracting many international companies. The financial services sector employs just under a million workers but still has room for growth.

Tourism continues to be a major employer, contributing to just over 800,000 full time and part time jobs. The creation of a new high-speed train line prior to the recession has opened up many new markets and tourist destinations.

Despite growth in some areas, unemployment remains a key issue.

Crime rates are fairly low in Pimlico compared to other G20 countries. However, there has been an increase in some violent crime as well as property crime recently. Cyber crime has also risen but, generally speaking, Pimlico is a safe place to live.

Part E Question 15 (continued)

SOURCE 2 Candidates' statements

Hilary Kennedy, Freedom Party

This election is an important one for our nation. It is one in which we have to make the right choices. The right choices for our economy. If elected, I will guarantee that I will look after and grow our economy. I will create jobs. Safe, secure jobs in banking by attracting the biggest banks and insurance companies to Pimlico.

I'll also stop the introduction of charges for our healthcare. The health of our nation is far too important to attach a price tag. Healthcare should be based on need. If elected, I'll make sure that free healthcare remains exactly that.

As voters, I know that you are worried about terrorism and want to see me do something about it. And rightly so. The safety and security of our citizens is our key objective and, if elected, I will protect the people of Pimlico from the very real threat of terrorism.

Vote Hilary!

Ben Curtis, Liberty Party

We have had a tough couple of years. Our economy went into recession and we are only beginning to see the green shoots of recovery. We need to focus on all areas of the economy, however, the key to the future success of Pimlico is based on tourism not terrorism. If elected, I will put tourism as the key focus of our economic strategy.

We also need to tackle crime in our cities. Some crime figures are growing and I know that it is a concern of voters. Feeling safe in our cities is as important to me as it is to you. I will put more police on the streets to protect you and your property.

I will be tough on immigration. I will make it harder for immigrants to come to Pimlico. We welcome their contribution but enough is enough. Increased immigration costs real jobs and I will introduce a cap on the number of immigrants while we are still in recession. I will review this passport to Pimlico policy once the recession is over.

Vote Ben!

B

SOURCE 3

Opinion poll on voters' main election priorities

Question: What issues are important in the Pimlico presidential election?

Issue	Yes	No
Health	65%	35%
Jobs	92%	8%
Immigration	22%	78%
Defence	67%	33%
Economy	86%	14%
Law and order	61%	39%
Terrorism	31%	69%
Tourism	78%	22%

MARKS

You must decide which option to recommend, **either** Hilary Kennedy (Option 1) **or** Ben Curtis (Option 2).

(i)   Using Sources 1, 2 and 3, **which option would you choose**?

(ii) Give reasons to **support** your choice.

(iii) **Explain** why you did not choose the other option.

Your answer must be based on all **three** sources.

10

Part F – World Issues

In your answers to Questions 16 and 17 you should give recent examples from a world issue you have studied.

Question 16

International issues or conflicts impact on individual nations.

Describe, **in detail, two** ways in which an international issue or conflict you have studied impacts on individual nations.

4

Question 17

Some people believe that international organisation/s have had limited success in tackling a world issue or conflict.

Explain, **in detail**, why some people believe that international organisation/s have had limited success in tackling a world issue or conflict you have studied.

6

B

Question 18

Study Sources 1, 2 and 3 and then answer the question which follows.

You have to choose which candidate you think would be the best choice as General Secretary of the African Union.

Option 1	Option 2
Benjamin Charles	Amara Lahoud

SOURCE 1

Factfile on the African Union

On 25 May 1963 in Addis Ababa, Ethiopia, the 32 African states that had achieved independence at that time agreed to establish the Organisation of African Unity (OAU). A further 21 members joined gradually, reaching a total of 53 by the time of the AU's creation in 2002. On 9 July 2011, South Sudan became the 54th African Union (AU) member.

The African Union's main objectives are to promote the unity and solidarity of African states; co-ordinate and intensify their co-operation and efforts to achieve a better life for the peoples of Africa; safeguard the sovereignty and territorial integrity of member states; rid the continent of colonisation and apartheid; promote international co-operation within the United Nations framework; and harmonise members' political, diplomatic, economic, educational, cultural, health, welfare, scientific, technical and defence policies.

Africa continues to suffer from issues such as poor healthcare, increased terrorism, lack of democracy and poor development. The ongoing issues of civil war and HIV/AIDS are also significant issues.

In sub-Saharan Africa, 25 million people have HIV/AIDS and 15 per cent of 25-year-olds in that region have the virus. Over 1 million people die per year and, in 2015, there were 1.5 million new cases.

Sub-Saharan Africa averages 1.15 health workers for every 1,000 of its citizens. A severe shortage of nurses and midwives means that over two-thirds of women in sub-Saharan Africa have no contact with health personnel following childbirth. Therefore, Africa accounts for more than half of the world's maternal and child deaths.

Only 9 of the 54 member nations of the African Union have some form of democratically elected government.

Terrorism is on the rise in Africa. In 2013, terrorist groups were successful in carrying out attacks in many African countries. In May of 2013, a terrorist group, Boko Haram attacked an army barracks and police station in Nigeria. Groups such as Al Shabab and AQIM have also been responsible for terrorist attacks in many African Union countries.

Part F Question 18 (continued)

SOURCE 2 Candidates' statements

Benjamin Charles

This election is a very important one for the African Union. It is one which will decide the future direction that we will take. My priorities, if elected, are clear. I want to improve the lives of all African citizens. I have been involved with the African Union for many years and know what issues matter.

I know what is important. Healthcare is a major issue. We need to build more hospitals and train more doctors and nurses. This is one of my priorities.

In tackling poor healthcare, we should also look at finally eradicating HIV/AIDS. Too many of our fellow citizens are dying. We need to sit down with the drugs companies and work out a way of helping those with this awful virus. Terrorism is not an issue for many Africans. What really matters is dealing with HIV/AIDS and fixing our healthcare.

A vote for me will ensure this happens.

Amara Lahoud

This election matters because people matter. The future direction of the African Union is at stake here. We must make sure that we take the right decisions and make the right choices. I have been involved in working with the African Union and the people of this great continent for many years so I know what issues are the important ones.

We, firstly, need to bring more democracy to our continent. People need to have their voices heard. More citizens need to be involved in the decision making process. If elected, I will promote fair elections within our member nations.

We also need to tackle, head on, the growing problem of terrorism. We need to keep our citizens safe from harm. We need to take the fight to the terrorists. If elected, I will create an African Union Task Force to take the fight to these terrorist groups. We will defeat them.

Issues such as HIV/AIDS are no longer the main issues for the majority of Africans in the 21st century. The real issues now are promoting democracy and defeating terrorism. I am the best candidate to do these things.

Part F Question 18 (continued)

SOURCE 3

Opinion poll

Question: What issues do you consider to be important?

Issue	Yes	No	Don't know
Healthcare	76%	18%	6%
More democracy	54%	30%	16%
Terrorism	76%	10%	14%
HIV/AIDS	50%	47%	3%
Civil war	37%	59%	4%
Trade/Aid	45%	45%	10%

MARKS

You must decide which option to recommend, **either** Benjamin Charles (Option 1) **or** Amara Lahoud (Option 2).

(i) Using Sources 1, 2 and 3, **which option would you choose**?

(ii) Give reasons to **support** your choice.

(iii) Explain why you did not choose the other option.

Your answer must be based on all **three** sources.

10

[END OF PRACTICE PAPER B]

National 5 Modern Studies

HODDER
GIBSON
LEARN MORE

Duration: 1 hour and 30 minutes

Total marks: 60

SECTION 1 – DEMOCRACY IN SCOTLAND AND THE UNITED KINGDOM – 20 marks

Attempt ONE part, EITHER

Part A Democracy in Scotland	Pages 45–47
OR	
Part B Democracy in the United Kingdom	Pages 48–50

SECTION 2 – SOCIAL ISSUES IN THE UNITED KINGDOM – 20 marks

Attempt ONE part, EITHER

Part C Social Inequality	Pages 51–53
OR	
Part D Crime and the Law	Pages 54–56

SECTION 3 – INTERNATIONAL ISSUES – 20 marks

Attempt ONE part, EITHER

Part E World Powers	Pages 57–58
OR	
Part F World Issues	Pages 59–61

Before attempting the questions you must check that your answer booklet is for the same subject and level as this question paper.

Read the questions carefully.

On the answer booklet, you must clearly identify the question number you are attempting.

Use **blue** or **black** ink.

Before leaving the examination room you must give your answer booklet to the Invigilator. If you do not, you may lose all the marks for this paper.

Section 1

SECTION 1 – DEMOCRACY IN SCOTLAND AND THE UNITED KINGDOM – 20 marks

Attempt ONE part, EITHER

Part A Democracy in Scotland   Pages 45–47

OR

Part B Democracy in the United Kingdom   Pages 48–50

Part A – Democracy in Scotland

MARKS

In your answers to Questions 1 and 2 you should give recent examples from Scotland.

Question 1

Apart from voting, there are many ways that people can participate during elections in Scotland.

Describe, **in detail**, **two** ways apart from voting that people can participate during elections in Scotland.

6

Question 2

Citizens in Scotland should use their vote.

Explain, **in detail**, **two** reasons why citizens in Scotland should use their vote.

6

C

Part A (continued)

Question 3

Study Sources 1, 2 and 3 and then answer the question which follows.

SOURCE 1

Elections overview

There are many ways for Scottish voters to participate in the democratic process. Not only are they able to vote for their MP and MSPs, they can also vote for who they want to represent them in their local authority and also in the European Parliament. In addition to this, Scottish voters can also take part in single question referenda such as the Scottish Independence vote in September 2014. Clearly, there are no shortages of democratic opportunities for Scots to participate in the decision making processes of the nation.

The number of people turning out to vote varies according to the type of election. Some elections are more likely to have a higher turnout than others. However, voter turnout has been steadily decreasing since the 1950s. Recently, in some elections, voter turnout has been less than 40 per cent in some areas. The lack of engagement in the political process by some voters is a worrying trend that could become a major issue.

Across all elections, clear patterns emerge in terms of voter turnout. A person's age, their position in society, their gender as well as their ethnicity and geographical location have an influence, not just on who they vote for but also whether they actually vote or not. The more prosperous you are, the more likely you are to vote. Better off and wealthier Scottish citizens in social groups ABC1 are more likely vote than poorer Scots in groups C2DE. Likewise with age. There are clear differences between the turnout of younger and older voters. The votes of older voters are often very influential in deciding the outcome of elections. For many political parties, getting young voters to the polling station is a serious problem.

SOURCE 2

Turnout in Scotland and type of election

Type of election	Turnout
Local council election 2012	39.1%
General election 2015	71.1%
Scottish Parliamentary election 2011	50.4%
European Parliamentary election 2014	33.5%
Scottish Independence Referendum 2014	85.0%

Part A Question 3 (continued)

SOURCE 3 Selected referendum statistics

Election statistics – turnout by selected characteristic

Scottish Independence Referendum

Age	Turnout
16–34	73%
35–54	87%
55 and over	92%

Gender	Turnout
Male	83%
Female	86%

Social group	Turnout
ABC1	88%
C2DE	79%

Using Sources 1, 2 and 3, what **conclusions** can be drawn about voter turnout?

MARKS

You should reach a conclusion about each of the following:

- age and voter turnout
- social group and voter turnout
- type of election and voter turnout.

Your conclusions **must** be supported by evidence from the sources. You should link information within and between the sources in support of your conclusions.

Your answer must be based on all **three** sources.

8

[NOW GO TO SECTION 2 ON PAGE 51]

Part B – Democracy in the United Kingdom

In your answers to Questions 4 and 5 you should give recent examples from the United Kingdom.

Question 4

> Apart from voting, there are many ways that people can participate during elections in the United Kingdom.

Describe, **in detail**, **two** ways apart from voting that people can participate during elections in the United Kingdom.

6

Question 5

> Citizens in the United Kingdom should use their vote.

Explain, **in detail**, **two** reasons why citizens in the United Kingdom should use their vote.

6

Part B (continued)

Question 6

Study Sources 1, 2 and 3 and then answer the question which follows.

SOURCE 1

Elections overview

There are many ways for UK voters to participate in the democratic process. Not only are they able to vote for their MP, they can also vote for who they want to represent them in their local authority and also in the European Parliament. In addition to this, English voters can also take part in elections for local mayors. Londoners can also vote for members to their assembly. Clearly, there are no shortages of democratic opportunities for UK voters to participate in the decision making processes of the nation.

The number of people turning out to vote varies according to the type of election. Some elections are more likely to have a higher turnout than others. However, voter turnout has been steadily decreasing since the 1950s. Recently, in some elections, voter turnout has been less than 40 per cent in some areas. The lack of engagement in the political process by some voters is a worrying trend that could become a major issue.

Across all elections, clear patterns emerge in terms of voter turnout. A person's age, their position in society, their gender as well as their ethnicity and geographical location have an influence not just on who they vote for but also whether they actually vote or not. The more prosperous you are, the more likely you are to vote. Better off and wealthier UK citizens in social groups ABC1 are more likely vote than poorer voters in groups C2DE. Likewise with age. There are clear differences between the turnout of younger and older voters. The votes of older voters are often very influential in deciding the outcome of elections. For many political parties, getting young voters to the polling station is a serious problem.

SOURCE 2

Turnout and type of election

Type of election	Turnout
Local council election 2012	31.3%
General Election 2015	67.0%
London mayoral election	37.4%
European Parliamentary election 2014	35.6%

Part B Question 6 (continued)

SOURCE 3

Election statistics – turnout by selected characteristic

UK General Election 2015

Age	Turnout
16–34	49%
35–54	68%
55 and over	77%

Gender	Turnout
Male	67%
Female	66%

Social group	Turnout
ABC1	72%
C2DE	59%

MARKS

Using Sources 1, 2 and 3, what **conclusions** can be drawn about the voter turnout?

You should reach a conclusion about each of the following:

- age and voter turnout
- social group and voter turnout
- type of election and voter turnout.

Your conclusions **must** be supported by evidence from the sources. You should link information within and between the sources in support of your conclusions.

Your answer must be based on all **three** sources.

8

[NOW GO TO SECTION 2 ON PAGE 51]

SECTION 2 – SOCIAL ISSUES IN THE UNITED KINGDOM – 20 marks

Attempt ONE part, EITHER

Part C Social Inequality   Pages 51–53

OR

Part D Crime and the Law   Pages 54–56

Part C – Social Inequality

MARKS

*In your answers to Questions 7 and 8 you should give recent examples
from the United Kingdom.*

Question 7

Social inequality exists in the United Kingdom.

Describe, **in detail**, **two** ways in which social inequality exists in the
United Kingdom.   4

Question 8

Some people think that attempts to tackle social inequality have been successful.

Explain, **in detail**, **two** reasons why some people think that attempts to
tackle social inequality have been successful.   6

C

Part C (continued)

Question 9

Study Sources 1, 2 and 3 and then answer the question which follows.

You have been asked to decide whether the Government should raise the drinking age to 25 in order to tackle alcohol abuse.

Option 1	Option 2
Change the law so people have to be 25 to buy alcohol.	Keep the law as it is. No change.

SOURCE 1

Factfile on alcohol in Scotland

- 84% of Scots thought alcohol causes either a 'great deal' or 'quite a lot' of harm in Scotland.
- Most people disapprove of excessive drinking – only 19% thought that 'getting drunk is a perfectly acceptable thing to do on weekends'.
- 42% of men and 43% of women correctly identified the recommended daily consumption limits for their gender.
- Nearly 1 in 4 men (23%) and around 1 in 6 women (17%) drink at harmful or hazardous levels (defined as drinking more than 14 units per week).
- Studies have shown that those who drink alcohol at an earlier age are more likely to develop alcohol-related issues in later life than those don't.
- The proportion of 15-year-olds who had recently drunk alcohol fell to 19% in 2013, down from 34% in 2010.
- There were 1,152 alcohol-related deaths in 2014.
- Alcohol deaths in Scotland are almost double those in the early 1990s.
- 482 deaths were people aged 45–59, 395 deaths in the 60–74 age group, 146 deaths in the 30–44 age group, and smaller numbers for other age groups.
- The 45–59 age group has had the largest number of alcohol-related deaths in almost every year since 1979.

SOURCE 2

Opinions on the proposed change in the law

View 1 – 'A great idea. Everyone benefits.'

Alcohol is a major issue in Scotland. Many Scots have issues with the abuse of alcohol and it is a significant factor in the poor health statistics of our nation. Something needs to be done about it. We need to tackle the problem. Drastic problems need drastic solutions. The public think that the Government should do more to tackle our alcohol crisis in Scotland. We need to increase the legal age to buy alcohol to 25.

Currently, young men are the most likely group to have alcohol-related stays in hospital. Not only that, the number of alcohol-related deaths in Scotland is a very big worry. We need to target young people to get them to change their habits and behaviour when it comes to alcohol. Changing the law to 25 years of age would make it harder for young people to get alcohol. This would improve their health and decrease the chance of alcohol-related problems over the course of their life.

Part C Question 9 (continued)

Young people's bodies are more vulnerable than adults' to the effects of alcohol. The brain continues to develop into the early twenties and introducing this change in the law would lead to greater health benefits for the individual and better health statistics for the nation.

A Senior Health Professional

View 2 'A stupid and silly idea. It'll do more harm than good.'

'Yes, Scotland does have an historic issue with alcohol. I can't deny that. Too many Scots have paid the price of poor health and a shorter life due to their excess alcohol consumption. Many still do but changing the law and increasing the age to buy alcohol to 25 is not the correct solution. It targets the wrong people. Younger people are making better lifestyle choices about alcohol than previous generations. Many are choosing not to drink alcohol in their teens and this is being carried forward into their early twenties. The ban is unnecessary.

It also targets the wrong groups. Government should focus its attention onto those other groups that are more likely to suffer serious health issues due to the alcohol misuse. That would be more effective than punishing all young people by increasing the age.

Many young people do know the risks and act accordingly around alcohol. It is unfair to punish all young people for the wrong lifestyle choices of a relatively few young people who drink to excess.

Current strategies are working. The messages around cutting back and staying within a safe limit are getting through. The majority of Scots do know what their daily consumption rates should be and this shows that previous campaigns and strategies are working. We don't need this unnecessary law change. Improvements are already occurring.

Spokesperson for the Scottish Licensed Trade

SOURCE 3

Opinion poll

1 Should the Scottish Government do more to tackle alcohol abuse?

Yes	67%	No	27%	Don't know	6%

2 What measures should the Scottish Government introduce to tackle alcohol abuse?
■ More health promotional campaigns?

Yes	62%	No	30%	Don't know	8%

■ Increase age to buy alcohol?

Yes	48%	No	48%	Don't know	4%

■ Increase tax on alcohol?

Yes	19%	No	75%	Don't know	6%

■ Limit the number of bar and pub licences?

Yes	15%	No	78%	Don't know	7%

You must decide which option to recommend, **either** change the law (Option 1) **or** keep the law as it is (Option 2).

MARKS

(i) Using Sources 1, 2 and 3, **which option would you choose**?

(ii) Give reasons to **support** your choice.

(iii) Explain why you did not choose the other option.

Your answer must be based on all **three** sources.

10

[NOW GO TO SECTION 3 ON PAGE 57]

C

Part D – Crime and the Law

In your answers to Questions 10 and 11 you should give recent examples from the United Kingdom.

Question 10

Those in wealthier social groups also commit crimes.

Describe, **in detail**, **two** types of crime that those in wealthier social groups are more likely to commit.

4

Question 11

Social deprivation can cause crime.

Explain, **in detail**, **two** reasons why social deprivation can cause crime.

6

C

Part D (continued)

Question 12

Study Sources 1, 2 and 3 and then answer the question which follows.

You have been asked to decide whether the Government should raise the drinking age to 25 in order to tackle violent crime.

Option 1	Option 2
Change the law so people have to be 25 to buy alcohol.	Keep the law as it is. No change.

SOURCE 1

Factfile on crime and alcohol

- In 6 out of 10 cases (59%) of violent crime, the victim said the offender was under the influence of alcohol.
- In the past 10 years, half of those accused of murder were under the influence of alcohol and/or drugs at the time of the murder.
- Two-thirds of young offenders were drunk at the time of their offence.
- Overall costs of alcohol misuse in Scotland are estimated to be £3.5bn with alcohol-related crime accounting for over £700m.
- In the UK, alcohol-related crime and social disorder is estimated to cost the UK taxpayer between £8 billion and £11 billion per year.
- 22% of violent crime happened in or around a pub, bar or club and 46% occurred at the weekend between 6 p.m. and 6 a.m.
- In around half of all violent incidents (52%), the offender was believed to be between 16 and 24 years old.
- According to the Scottish Crime Survey, violent crime in Scotland fell 20% between 2012 and 2013.
- 1,000 underage drinkers are taken to hospital each year in Scotland. 35% of Scottish school pupils drink to excess between the ages of 14 and 17.

SOURCE 2

Views on crime and alcohol

View 1 – 'The Government must tackle alcohol-related violent crime.'

There is a clear link between alcohol, young people and violent crime. Alcohol causes violent crime with young people being the main offender when it comes to this type of crime. Too many young people drink too much and end up getting into fights and disturbances. This must stop. It is clear that the Government must act now before our streets and town centres become no-go areas for law abiding people. The public believe that the Government must do something. Increasing the age to purchase alcohol is popular with voters and the government should consider this option.

This proposal makes sense. By restricting the sale of alcohol, the Government is sending a strong message that it takes the issue very seriously.

By increasing the age to buy alcohol, the Government will be cutting the likelihood of young adults getting drunk and getting into fights. This policy makes sense. The Government should introduce the increase of the age to buy alcohol to 25. It will cut violent crime and make our streets safer.

A Criminal Justice Advisor

Part D Question 12 (continued)

View 2 'Unworkable and unnecessary.'

Yes, violent crime on our streets is an issue. And yes, too many violent crimes are caused by young people getting drunk and into fights but this proposed law is unnecessary. Violent crime is an issue but we have turned the corner on violent crime. We are beginning to crack it. The statistics are very encouraging and it shows that what the Government is doing is correct and that we shouldn't go changing things.

The proposal to increase the age to buy alcohol to 25 years of age is a policy that won't work. Under 25s will still drink alcohol. They will just get someone to buy it for them. Even with a ban on under 18s buying alcohol, the hospital admission figures show that many underage drinkers still manage to obtain alcohol. The same thing will happen if this proposal is introduced. Members of the public are happy with what the government is doing in relation to tackling violent crime. This proposal will do nothing to cut it.

Member of the Youth Parliament

SOURCE 3

Opinion poll

1   Do you think the Government should do more to tackle violent crime?

Yes	73%	No	18%	Don't know	9%

2   What should the Government do to tackle violent crime?
   - More police on the streets?

Yes	68%	No	26%	Don't know	6%

   - More CCTV?

Yes	47%	No	42%	Don't know	11%

   - Increase age to buy alcohol to 25?

Yes	48%	No	48%	Don't know	4%

   - Longer prison sentences?

Yes	63%	No	34%	Don't know	3%

You must decide which option to recommend, **either** change the law (Option 1) **or** keep the law as it is (Option 2).

MARKS

(i)   Using Sources 1, 2 and 3, **which option would you choose**?

(ii)   Give reasons to **support** your choice.

(iii) **Explain** why you did not choose the other option.

Your answer must be based on all **three** sources.

10

[NOW GO TO SECTION 3 ON PAGE 57]

SECTION 3 – INTERNATIONAL ISSUES – 20 marks

Attempt ONE part, EITHER

Part E World Powers   Pages 57–58

OR

Part F World Issues   Pages 59–61

Part E – World Powers

MARKS

In your answers to Questions 13 and 14 you should give recent examples from a world power you have studied.

Question 13

World powers have tried to tackle socio-economic issues in their country.

Describe, **in detail**, **two** ways that the world power you have studied has tried to tackle socio-economic issues in their country.

In your answer you should state the world power you have studied.   6

Question 14

Many world powers can claim to have a global influence.

Explain, **in detail**, **two** reasons the world power you have studied can claim to have a global influence.

In your answer you should state the world power you have studied.   6

Part E (continued)

Question 15

Study Sources 1, 2 and 3 and then answer the question which follows.

SOURCE 1

> ## Factfile on the European Union
>
> - The main aims of the European Union are to promote economic and social progress and to develop Europe as an area of freedom, security and justice.
> - Membership is open to any country with a democratic government, a good human rights record, and sound economic policies. It currently has 27 member nations.
> - Albania, Iceland, Macedonia, Montenegro, Serbia and Turkey have applied to join the EU.
> - An estimated 507 million people lived within the European Union in 2014.
> - Following the recession, there were anti-European Union riots in Athens in protest at the EU's role in increasing poverty in Greece.
> - 19 European Union members have adopted the euro as their currency.
> - Being a member of the European Union allows EU citizens the right to live and work in other member nations.

SOURCE 2

> ## European opinion poll
>
> **Do you feel favourable towards the European Union?**
>
> Percentage answering 'yes'
>
> | Country | 2013 | 2014 | Percentage change |
> |---------|------|------|-------------------|
> | France | 41 | 54 | +13 |
> | Germany | 60 | 66 | +6 |
> | Poland | 68 | 72 | +4 |
> | Italy | 58 | 46 | −12 |

SOURCE 3

> ## UK referendum on membership of the EU
>
> **Should the UK remain a member of the European Union or leave the European Union?**
>
> | | Remain | Leave | Don't know |
> |---|--------|-------|------------|
> | **Scottish voters** | 60% | 35% | 5% |
> | **English voters** | 44% | 46% | 10% |

Using Sources 1, 2 and 3, explain why the view of Isobel Porter **is selective in the use of facts**.

> European citizens are happy with the European Union.
>
> **View of Isabel Porter**

MARKS

In your answer you must:

- give evidence from the sources that support Isabel Porter's view

and

- give evidence from the sources that oppose Isabel Porter's view.

Your answer must be based on all **three** sources.

8

Part F – World Issues

In your answers to Questions 16 and 17 you should give recent examples from a world issue you have studied.

Question 16

An issue or conflict in one country or area can have an impact on the wider international community.

Describe, **in detail**, **two** ways in which an issue or conflict in one country or area can have an impact on the wider international community.

6

Question 17

International organisations attempt to resolve world issues or conflicts.

Explain, **in detail**, **two** reasons why international organisations attempt to resolve world issues or conflicts.

6

Part F (continued)

Question 18

Study Sources 1, 2 and 3 and then answer the question which follows.

SOURCE 1

Factfile

- Organisations such as the United Nations (UN), the European Union (EU), the African Union (AU) and the North Atlantic Treaty Organisation (NATO) try to tackle world issues.
- The United Nations works with its agencies in the developing world to tackle issues such as famine, poor mortality and morbidity rates and promote democracy and better education.
- The European Union was formed to promote economic and social progress within its members. It aims to promote peace and co-operation.
- The African Union works to promote economic development across Africa. It works to reduce HIV/AIDS in sub-Saharan Africa.
- NATO members have been involved in the Middle East in countries such as Iraq, Afghanistan and Syria.
- NATO has been working with its member countries to tackle international terrorism.
- The United Nations' headquarters is in New York and there are five permanent members of the Security Council. These are the USA, Russia, China, France and the United Kingdom.

SOURCE 2

News report

Our correspondent reports that more than 7 million people are now receiving HIV treatment across Africa – with nearly 1 million added in the last year – while new HIV infections and deaths from AIDS continue to fall.

In other news, police in Athens had to use tear gas and water cannon today to disperse rioters who had been gathering next to the Parliament building. This is the third week of protests in the Greek capital as protestors have taken to the streets in protest at the EU-imposed cuts that have hit many millions of Greek workers, pensioners and the unemployed very hard. Unemployment is now 30 per cent.

This is Kate Jones for Network News.

Part F Question 18 (continued)

SOURCE 3

Selected statistics

	Year 2012	Year 2013	Year 2014
Number of terrorist attacks	6,771	9,964	13,436
Infant mortality per 1,000 (Africa)	78	68	57
Countries with the death penalty	45	41	37
Number of refugees	14m	16.5m	19.2m
Unemployment in Greece	11%	20%	30%

Using Sources 1, 2 and 3, explain why the view of **Martin Santini is selective in the use of facts**.

International organisations are effective at tackling world issues.

View of Martin Santini

In your answer you must:

MARKS

■ give evidence from the sources that support Martin Santini's view

and

■ give evidence from the sources that oppose Martin Santini's view.

Your answer must be based on all **three** sources.

8

[END OF PRACTICE PAPER C]

National 5 Modern Studies

Practice Paper A

Section 1

Part A

1 Candidates can be credited in a number of ways **up to a maximum of 4 marks**.

Possible approaches to answering the question:

- An important power of the First Minister is that they are the political leader of Scotland and head of the Scottish government.

  1 mark – accurate but undeveloped point.

- Nicola Sturgeon is Scotland's First Minister. She has the important power to appoint MSPs to key posts in her cabinet. John Swinney is deputy First Minister and is the cabinet secretary in charge of education.

  2 marks – accurate point with development.

- An important power of Nicola Sturgeon is that she represents Scotland on the world stage and although it is a reserved power she can outline Scottish Government's defence and foreign policy. She is opposed to Trident and UK air strikes on Syria. In December 2015, she attended the Paris Summit on climate change as part of the UK delegation but also as a member of the Compact of States and Regions.

  3 marks – accurate point with development and exemplification.

Credit reference to aspects of the following:

- Leader of the Scottish Government.
- Directs policy in the Scottish Government.
- Spokesperson for the Scottish Government.
- Chairs Scottish Cabinet meetings.
- Chooses members of the Scottish Cabinet.
- Leader of the biggest party in the Scottish Parliament.
- Takes part in First Minister's Question Time every week.
- Lead role in discussions with other devolved governments and overseas.
- Focus of media attention.

Any other valid point that meets the criteria described in the general marking instructions.

2 Candidates can be credited in a number of ways **up to a maximum of 6 marks**.

Possible approaches to answering the question:

- Some people do not vote because they are not on the electoral register.

  1 mark – accurate but undeveloped point.

- One reason some people do not vote is that they do not trust politicians because of recent scandals. They also feel it will make no difference to their lives and do not see the point.

  2 marks – accurate point with development.

- One reason some people do not vote is that they think politicians are out of touch with the public and are only involved in politics for personal gain. Recently, MSPs received a pay rise well above the rate of inflation. Yet public sector workers were only given a one per cent wage rise. So this unfairness makes the public even more disillusioned.

  3 marks – accurate point with development and exemplification.

Credit reference to aspects of the following:

- Those who support minority parties are aware that their party will win no seats even with the Additional Member System (AMS).
- There has been a steady decline in the number of voters who join a political party, so more and more of the public are not interested in mainstream politics.
- Increase in the number of people joining pressure groups and supporting single issue actions.
- Not everyone can vote which includes Scottish prisoners and those not on the electoral list.
- Voter apathy is increasing.
- Opinion polls show trust in politicians is declining.
- A significant number of people under the age of 25 do not vote.

Any other valid point that meets the criteria described in the general marking instructions.

3 Candidates can be credited in a number of ways **up to a maximum of 10 marks**.

Possible approaches to answering the question:

For Option 1:

- I would recommend Lucas Watt as he is a schoolteacher with experience in education.
  1 mark – evidence drawn from Source 1.

- In Source 1 Lucas Watt says that parents are concerned about the future education of their children. He is right as the educational services will not be able to cope with the increase in population.
  2 marks – evaluative terminology with limited evidence.

- In Source 1 Lucas Watt supports the housing development as 'it will provide new facilities for Linburn' and 'provide lots of jobs for the area'. It will also bring in more council tax. He is correct as Source 2 indicates that a community centre, leisure centre and primary school will be built and that an industrial site is being built already – all significant developments.
  3 marks – detailed evidence drawn from two sources with evaluative terminology.

Reference to aspects of the following will be credited:

- 'Creation of a new industrial estate will provide employment opportunities for all' (Source 1).
- Supports an increase in council tax to protect local services and to increase revenue (Source 1).
- Supports the immediate building of a second primary school and expansion of the secondary school (Source 1).
- The massive private housing development will eventually double the population (Source 2).
- The local secondary school has a very good reputation with high standards (Source 2).
- 40% of school leavers have 3 or more Highers compared to 30% in Scotland as a whole (Source 2).
- A majority of 54% believe the housing development is good for Linburn (Source 3).
- 58% agree that a new primary school is a priority for Linburn (Source 3).

Against Option1:

- 'We have a low crime rate and we cannot justify the reopening of the police station' (Source 1) but Source 3 shows 52% of the Linburn public disagree.
  2 marks – evaluative terminology with limited evidence.

- Many Linburn residents are concerned about the growing crime rate. Frank Clark believes they need a stronger police presence (Source 2).
  2 marks – evaluative terminology with limited evidence.

Reference to aspects of the following will be credited:

- Supports an increase in council tax to protect local services (Source 1) – however, 80% of residents own their own homes and are concerned that council taxes might rise (Source 2).
- Also, in Source 3, a majority of 55% do not want council taxes to be increased.

For Option 2:

- I would choose Sophie Willis as she is against an increase in council tax and Source 3 shows that in the survey of public opinion 55% are against an increase in the council tax.
  2 marks – evidence drawn from Sources 1 and 3.
- In Source 1, Sophie Willis states that 'our most urgent priority is health provision'. She is correct as in Source 3 a majority (58%) believe that a second health centre is a priority.
  2 marks – evidence drawn from Sources 1 and 3.
- In Source 1, Sophie Willis states that crime is a major concern in the area 'and she will fight for the restoration of our police station'. She is correct as many people, especially the elderly, feel vulnerable. In Source 2 Frank Clark, Chair of the Community Council, indicates that there has been an increase in house break-ins and more and more residents are contacting him with their worries and concerns and demanding a greater police presence.
  3 marks – detailed evidence drawn from two sources with evaluative terminology.

Against Option 2:

- The schools can easily cope with the increase in demand (Source 1) but Source 2 shows that the population will double and Source 3 shows 58% of the Linburn public want a new primary school (2 marks).

Reference to aspects of the following will be credited:

- In Source 1, Sophie Willis is against any increase to the council tax. However, some accept the need for an increase if it prevents cuts to education and community health (Source 2).
- Sophie Willis states in Source 1 that schools can cope and that education is not a priority. However, in Source 3, 58% regard education as a priority.
- Sophie Willis is against the housing development (Source 1). However, in Source 3, 54% state that the housing development is good for Linburn.

Part B

4 Candidates can be credited in a number of ways **up to a maximum of 4 marks**.

Possible approaches to answering the question:

- An important power of the Prime Minister is that they are the political leader of the UK and head of the UK government.

  1 mark – accurate but undeveloped point.

- David Cameron is Britain's Prime Minister. He has the important power to appoint MPs to key posts in his cabinet. George Osborne is deputy Prime Minister and is the Chancellor of the Exchequer and is in charge of the country's finances.

  2 marks – accurate point with development.

- An important power of David Cameron is that he represents the UK on the world stage and he can outline the UK Government's defence and foreign policy. He supports Trident and UK air strikes on Syria. In December 2015, he attended the Paris Summit on climate change as leader of the UK delegation.

  3 marks – accurate point with development and exemplification.

Credit reference to aspects of the following:

- Leader of the UK Government.
- Directs policy in the UK Government.
- Spokesperson for the UK Government.
- Chairs UK Cabinet meetings.
- Chooses members of the UK Cabinet.
- Leader of the biggest party in the UK Parliament.
- Takes part in Prime Minister's Question Time every week.
- Lead role in discussions with other governments around the world.
- Focus of media attention.

Any other valid point that meets the criteria described in the general marking instructions.

5 Candidates can be credited in a number of ways **up to a maximum of 6 marks**.

Possible approaches to answering the question:

- Some people do not vote because they are not on the electoral register.

  1 mark – accurate but undeveloped point.

- One reason some people do not vote is that they do not trust politicians because of recent scandals. They also feel it will make no difference to their lives and do not see the point.

  2 marks – accurate point with development.

- One reason some people do not vote is that they think politicians are out of touch with the public and are only involved in politics for personal gain. Recently, MPs received a pay rise well above the rate of inflation. Yet public sector workers were only given a one per cent wage rise. So this unfairness makes the public even more disillusioned.

  3 marks – accurate point with development and exemplification.

Credit reference to aspects of the following:

- Those who support minority parties are aware that their party will win no seats because of FPTP.
- There has been a steady decline in the number of voters who join a political party, so more and more of the public are not interested in mainstream politics.
- Increase in the number of people joining pressure groups and supporting single issue actions.
- Not everyone can vote which includes UK prisoners and those under the age of 18.
- Voter apathy is increasing.

- Opinion polls show trust in politicians is declining.
- A significant number of people under the age of 25 do not vote.

Any other valid point that meets the criteria described in the general marking instructions.

6 Candidates can be credited in a number of ways **up to a maximum of 10 marks**.

Possible approaches to answering the question:

For Option 1:

- I would choose Gemma Healy as she has the experience of being a social worker and will know about the impact of welfare cuts.

  1 mark – evidence drawn from Source 1.

- In Source 1, Gemma Healy says that women are under-represented across all senior management posts and we need more women MPs. She is right as almost 60% of the Inverbank public agree with her.

  2 marks – evaluative terminology with limited evidence.

- In Source 1, Gemma Healy states that she is 'against the welfare cuts' and that they will impact on the most vulnerable and needy in the community. She is completely correct as Source 2 indicates that Inverbank has a high deprivation index with life expectancy only 68, well below the UK average of 80.

  3 marks – detailed evidence drawn from two sources with evaluative terminology.

Reference to aspects of the following will be credited:

- Totally against the renewal of the Trident nuclear weapons programme, a waste of 'billions of pounds' and 52% of public opinion agree (Source 1).
- 'We pay too much into the EU' and 'we should leave the EU by voting 'No' in the forthcoming referendum' (Source 1).
- The number of people using foodbanks has doubled in the last 4 years (Source 2).
- Deprivation impacts on health indicators, with Inverbank having a greater number of people experiencing long-term health problems (21% compared to 18%) (Source 2).
- Over 70% of public opinion agrees that welfare cuts impact on the poor (Source 3).

Against Option 1:

- Gemma states that we should vote to leave the EU (Source 1) but Source 3 shows only 44% of the Inverbank public agree.

  2 marks – evaluative terminology with limited evidence.

Reference to aspects of the following will be credited:

- Supports the closure of the nuclear base at Faslane on the Clyde (Source 1), however, the Community Council is against the closure of Faslane as many workers will lose their jobs (Source 2).
- Also in Source 1, there is already a significantly higher rate of unemployed people claiming benefits – 20% compared to the Scottish average of 15%.
- Gemma wants to end the winter fuel allowance, however, Inverbank has a higher number of pensioners compared to other parts of Scotland.

For Option 2:

- I would choose Lewis Elliot as he has experience as a local councillor.

  1 mark – evidence drawn from Source 1.

- In Source 1, Lewis Elliot states that he will protect families and the elderly to maintain all their present benefits as poverty is an issue in Inverbank. He is right as the number of pensioners and those claiming benefits are significantly above the Scottish figures (Source 2).

  2 marks – evidence drawn from Sources 1 and 2.

- In Source 1, Lewis Elliot states that 'we need to attract new jobs to the area' and that too many people rely on state benefits to get by. He is correct as in Source 2 the percentage of people claiming benefits in Inverbank is higher than the Scottish figure (20% compared to 15%).The difference is significant and is worrying, especially for the school leavers with no qualifications (13% compared to 9%).

  3 marks – detailed evidence drawn from two sources with evaluative terminology.

Against Option 2:

- In Source 1, Lewis Elliot supports the Trident nuclear programme and the retention of Faslane. However, a majority of the public in Inverbank do not want it renewed and want the base closed (Source 2).

  2 marks – evaluative terminology with limited evidence.

Reference to aspects of the following will be credited:

- The party supports fairer gender representation in parliament and wants more women MPs – so Lewis Elliot should not be chosen.
- Again in Source 3, the opinion poll shows a clear majority for having more women MPs.

Section 2

Part C

7 Candidates can be credited in a number of ways **up to a maximum of 4 marks**.

Possible approaches to answering the question:

- One impact of living in poverty is that the child may suffer poorer health than other children who do not live in poverty.

  1 mark – accurate but undeveloped point.

- One impact of living in poverty is that these children may suffer poorer health than other children who do not live in poverty. Their homes may not be properly heated and be cold and damp.

  2 marks – accurate point with development.

- Children living in poverty may have a poor diet of cheap foods such as tinned or ready meals. They might not get a balanced diet as fruit and vegetables are expensive to buy and this can impact on their health.

  3 marks – accurate point with development and exemplification.

Credit reference to aspects of the following:

- ill health
- lack of material goods
- low self-esteem
- poor diet
- breakdown of family
- overcrowded/low standard of housing.

Any other valid point that meets the criteria described in the general marking instructions.

8 Candidates can be credited in a number of ways **up to a maximum of 8 marks**.

Possible approaches to answering the question:

- Health inequalities exist because many people still make poor lifestyle choices.

  1 mark – accurate but undeveloped point.

- Health inequalities exist because many people still make poor lifestyle choices. Choosing to smoke, excessively drinking alcohol and eating a poor diet can lead to serious health problems such as diabetes.

  2 marks – accurate point with development.

- There is a clear link between living in a poor area and having poorer health than someone who lives in a more affluent area. Living in poor housing with possible dampness, and lacking money to afford a balanced diet can damage one's health. Being unemployed can lead to depression and impact on health. In contrast, someone living in an affluent area is more likely to live in a warm house, eat a balanced diet and exercise.

  4 marks – accurate point with development and exemplification.

Credit reference to aspects of the following:

- Social and economic disadvantages – poor diet and effects of poverty.
- Lifestyle factors – effects of smoking, alcohol abuse and obesity.
- Geography and environment – poor quality housing, limited access to local amenities and impact of crime.

- Gender – women live longer than men but are more likely to suffer poor health.
- Ethnic minorities – high incidence of diabetes among Pakistanis and Indians. Also more likely to be poor and therefore to suffer poor health.

Any other valid point that meets the criteria described in the general marking instructions.

9 Candidates can be credited in a number of ways **up to a maximum of 8 marks**.

Possible approaches to answering the question:

Evidence to support the view of Ryan Wills:

- Sam Gunn feels that he is being exploited by his employer.

  1 mark – accurate use of Source 1 but minimal development.

- Sam Gunn feels that he is being exploited by his employer as in one week he might only work 8 hours but is not allowed to take another job.

  2 marks – accurate use of information from different parts of Source1.

- Sam Gunn feels that he is being exploited by his employer as he is not guaranteed set weekly hours so sometimes he has to use foodbanks as he does not have enough money. Over 40% of those on zero-hours contracts want more working hours compared to only 10% of workers on set contracts.

  3 marks – accurate use of information from Sources 1 and 2 with evaluative comment.

Reference to aspects of the following will be credited:

- Employers avoid redundancy payments and pension contributions (Source 1).
- In some months workers have to take out payday loans with high interest (Source 1).
- Gross weekly pay for zero-hours contracts is more than half compared to non zero-hours contracts and the hours worked are 21 hours compared to 33 hours (Source 3).

Evidence to oppose the view of Ryan Wills:

- Ryan is wrong as many workers are happy to have zero-hours contracts as it gives flexibility. Retired Michelle Kelly enjoys her contract as it brings in extra money and she still has time to see her grandchildren. So she does not feel exploited.

  2 marks – accurate use of Source 1 with evaluative comment.

- These contracts enable many workers to control their work–life balance – for example, it suits students who can combine their studies with earning money. This is supported in the survey of employment satisfaction where more people on zero-hours contracts feel they have the correct work–life balance (65% compared to 58%).

  2 marks – accurate use of information from Sources 1 and 2.

- Ryan is wrong as many workers are happy to have zero-hours contracts as it gives flexibility to retired workers and students – two examples of those who do not feel exploited. The elderly can enjoy earning more money by working part time but still have time to enjoy their retirement. In the survey on employment satisfaction the figure for zero-hours contracts is higher for work–life balance.

  3 marks – accurate use of information from Sources 1 and 2 with evaluative comment.

Reference to aspects of the following will be credited:

- For those who are retired this contract keeps them active (Source 1).
- In many cases both the employer and employee are happy with this contract (Source 1).
- 55% of those on a zero-hours contract do not want more hours (Source 2).

Part D

10 Candidates can be credited in a number of ways **up to a maximum of 4 marks**.

Possible approaches to answering the question:

- One type of crime that young people tend to commit is anti-social behaviour.

  1 mark – accurate but undeveloped point.

- A recent crime associated with young people is computer hacking. Many retail organisations have had their customers' details stolen. The average age of those charged with the crime is 17.

  2 marks – accurate point with development.

- Young people often commit anti-social behaviour. They may drink too much (illegal) alcohol and be hanging about housing estates or shops in gangs. Their behaviour is rowdy and can frighten the public, leading to police intervention.

  3 marks – accurate point with development and exemplification.

Credit reference to aspects of the following:

- shop lifting
- car theft
- vandalism
- breach of the peace
- graffiti
- computer hacking.

Any other valid point that meets the criteria described in the general marking instructions.

11 Candidates can be credited in a number of ways **up to a maximum of 8 marks**.

Possible approaches to answering the question:

- Prisons are not effective as too many prisoners reoffend when they come out of prison.

  1 mark – accurate but undeveloped point.

- Prisons are not effective as too many short-term prisoners reoffend when they come out of prison. With short sentences there is little opportunity for rehabilitation programmes.

  2 marks – accurate point with development.

- One reason is that Scotland's prisons are severely overcrowded and, with budget cuts, savings must be made. A community service punishment or a fine can be far more effective than handing out a short prison sentence. These types of sentences help to solve the issue of overcrowding in prisons. This will reduce the stress on prison officers and provide greater opportunities for rehabilitation programmes.

  4 marks – accurate point with development and exemplification.

Credit reference to aspects of the following:

- Prisons are expensive and overcrowded.
- High level of reoffending.
- Limited opportunities for rehabilitation.
- Non-custodial sentences keep families together.
- Non-custodial sentences can allow offenders to keep their jobs.
- Electronic tagging and Community Placements Orders are less expensive than prisons.
- Success of restorative justice especially for young people.

Any other valid point that meets the criteria described in the general marking instructions.

A

12 Candidates can be credited in a number of ways **up to a maximum of 8 marks**.

Possible approaches to answering the question:

Evidence to support the view of Catherine Daly:

- In the USA over 300 people have died after being tasered.

  1 mark – accurate use of Source 1 but minimal development.

- Innocent people and young people can be injured. For example, a blind man was tasered after the police officer thought he was carrying a dangerous weapon. Also, a 14-year-old boy was hit by a taser gun.

  2 marks – accurate use of information from Sources 1 and 2.

- Over 10,400 incidents were logged in the UK in 2014, including a 14-year-old boy being tasered. The human rights supporter argues that taser guns are a danger to the public and quotes evidence from the seriously high number of taser deaths in the USA.

  3 marks – accurate use of information from Sources 1 and 2 with evaluative comment.

Reference to aspects of the following will be credited:

- The British public have trust in their police and this trust may be damaged by the continual use of taser guns (Source 1).
- Increasing use of taser guns is of major concern (Source 2).
- Taser guns are a danger to the public (Source 2).
- Several men have died in England after being tasered (Source 2).
- Public opinion survey with over 60% agreeing that police might taser innocent citizens (Source 3).
- Public opinion survey with 50% agreeing that they are too dangerous (Source 3).

Evidence to oppose the view of Catherine Daly:

- Catherine is wrong as having a taser gun may defuse a possible threat to the public with the 'individual ending their aggressive behaviour'. In 2014, the police had to use a taser gun in only one out of five incidents. This shows that taser guns deter violent crime and protect the public.

  2 marks – accurate use of Source 1 with evaluative comment.

- A police officer in London is convinced that the use of taser guns protects not just the public but the police as well. This is supported in the survey of the police use of tasers with two-thirds of the public agreeing that their use will reduce violence against the police and public.

  2 marks – accurate use of information from Sources 1 and 3.

- Catherine is wrong as police use of taser guns is not a danger to all as their use can prevent serious injuries and save lives. The London police officer who almost died from a savage knife attack experienced serious injuries which could have been avoided if he had the protection of a taser gun. Officers go on a three-day training course and are properly trained. So the police make great efforts to ensure that the danger to the public is kept to a minimum.

  3 marks – accurate use of information from Sources 1 and 2 with evaluative comment.

Reference to aspects of the following will be credited:

- Any use of a taser gun must be recorded by the police and justified (Source 1).
- Tasers are an effective and non-lethal way of stopping a possible violent incident (Source1).
- Violent crime is rising and the life of a police officer is becoming more dangerous (Source 2).
- The police officer states: 'If I had a taser gun, I could have protected myself and the public.'
- A significant number of those surveyed would feel safer if the police had taser guns.

Section 3

Part E

13 Candidates can be credited in a number of ways **up to a maximum of 6 marks**.

Possible approaches to answering the question:

The USA

- One right American citizens have is to elect the President every four years.

  1 mark – accurate but undeveloped point.

- One right American citizens have is to elect the President every four years. Most Americans support either the Democratic Party or the Republican Party. The present President is Barak Obama, a Democrat.

  2 marks – accurate point with development.

- One right American citizens have is to stand for public office. At present Donald Trump is a leading candidate for the Republicans and Hilary Clinton for the Democrats. They have the right to express their political views but should be aware that they have a responsibility not to be extreme in their comments. Donald Trump wishes to stop any Muslim from entering America and this could lead to hate attacks on American Muslims. He is ignoring his responsibility as a leader.

  4 marks – accurate point with development, exemplification and analysis.

Credit reference to aspects of the following:

- The right to vote in local and national elections.
- The right to join a political party.
- The right to freedom of speech in public and online.
- The right to protest.
- The responsibility to turn out and use the vote.
- The responsibility to ensure peaceful protest and to stay within the law.
- The responsibility not to incite public violence.

Any other valid point that meets the criteria described in the general marking instructions.

China

- One right Chinese citizens have is to elect their representatives at the local level.

  1 mark – accurate but undeveloped point.

- One right Chinese citizens have is to be able to protest against local political decisions. However, they have the responsibility of only holding a protest if the Communist party approves of the protest.

  2 marks – accurate point with development.

- The Chinese Constitution grants the Chinese people many political rights but they are linked to the responsibilities of being loyal to the Communist party and its ideology. The people can only elect their representative at the local level. So many of these rights only seem to exist on paper, if they criticise the government or try to set up a new political party they will be arrested. Liu Xiabo, a Nobel Peace Prize winner, is in prison because he demanded political reforms.

  4 marks – accurate point with development, exemplification and analysis.

Credit reference to aspects of the following:

- The right to vote in local elections.
- The right to join the Communist party.
- The right to freedom of speech in public and online to strengthen Communism.
- The right to protest but only if permission is given.

- The responsibility to turn out and use the vote.
- The responsibility to ensure peaceful protest and to stay within the law.
- The responsibility not to incite public violence.

Any other valid point that meets the criteria described in the general marking instructions.

14 Candidates can be credited in a number of ways **up to a maximum of 6 marks**.

Possible approaches to answering the question:

South Africa

- In South Africa health inequalities still exist despite the introduction of a National Health Service.

  1 mark – accurate but undeveloped point.

- In South Africa the legacy of apartheid has created health inequalities between blacks and whites. Unemployment among blacks is about 40 per cent, while it is only 6 per cent for whites.

  2 marks – accurate point with development.

- Unemployment among blacks is estimated to be as high as 40 per cent with millions of black depending on government social grants for survival – over 13 million people receive these funds. The creation of a very wealthy black group, known as the Black Diamonds, has widened inequalities in South Africa. There are about 4 million Black Diamonds and many of them are millionaires.

  4 marks – accurate point with development, exemplification and analysis.

China

- In China there are inequalities between rural and urban areas.

  1 mark – accurate but undeveloped point.

- In China there are inequalities between the poor rural communities and the rich urban areas. In the rural areas most people work in low paid agricultural jobs and have a low standard of living. In contrast, many urban workers have highly paid employment working for the state or multi-national companies.

  2 marks – accurate point with development.

- In China there are vast inequalities in terms of housing, education and income between the migrant workers who come to the cities for work and those with a residence permit and middle class background. Migrant workers receive low pay and have to live in substandard homes. If they bring their families they will find it difficult to get them into schools. Middle class Chinese people have a high income and live in modern homes. Migrant workers are caught in the poverty trap.

  3 marks – accurate point with development, exemplification and analysis.

Credit reference to aspects of the following:

- educational inequalities
- issues relating to health and healthcare inequalities
- income and employment inequalities
- housing inequalities
- law and order issues.

Any other valid point that meets the criteria described in the general marking instructions.

15 Candidates can be credited in a number of ways **up to a maximum of 8 marks**.

Possible approaches to answering the question:

Electoral College results of 2012 election compared to 2008

Conclusion

In both elections Obama had a clear majority of the Electoral College votes but in the 2012 election the Republicans had increased their support and narrowed the difference.

1 mark – valid conclusion.

Evidence

In 2008, Obama received 365 votes (68%) with the Republican candidate winning 173 votes and in 2012 he had 126 more votes than the Republican candidate and received almost 62% of the votes (Sources 1 and 2).

2 marks – conclusion with evidence from two sources.

Popular vote results of 2012 election compared to 2008

Conclusion

In both elections Obama had a clear majority of the popular vote but in the 2012 election the Republicans had increased their support and narrowed the difference.

1 mark – valid conclusion.

Evidence

In 2008, Obama received 66 million votes but in 2012 he experienced a decline to 65 million votes with the Republican candidate increasing his party's share of the votes from just under 46% to 47%. Obama's percentage of votes fell by almost 2% (Sources 1 and 2).

2 marks – conclusion with evidence from two sources.

The link between age and ethnicity voting behaviour in the 2012 election

Conclusion

The elderly and whites were more likely to vote for the Republican candidate and the young and ethnic minorities more likely to vote for Obama.

1 mark – valid conclusion.

Evidence

There was a clear age and ethnic divide in voting. Those over the age of 50 favoured Romney with an 8 point difference. In contrast, Obama had a 12 point lead with the under 50 age group. There was a significant divide among the races with almost 60% of whites supporting the Republican candidate Romney and a staggering 93% of African-Americans supporting Obama (Sources 1 and 3).

2 marks – conclusion with evidence from two sources.

Part F

16 Candidates can be credited in a number of ways **up to a maximum of 6 marks**.

Possible approaches to answering the question:

- One cause of lack of development in Africa is corrupt governments.

  1 mark – accurate but undeveloped point.

- One cause of conflict in the Ukraine is that many citizens in Eastern Ukraine are of Russian origin and their loyalties are to Russia and not to the Ukraine Government.

  2 marks – accurate point with development.

- One cause of lack of development in Africa is conflict/civil war between different ethnic groups. After a long civil war, Sudan divided into two countries. Unfortunately the government in the new country of South Sudan failed to maintain peace and prosperity. The two main tribes that formed the coalition government began fighting and so ethnic rivalry and tension can lead to civil war.

  4 marks – accurate point with development, exemplification and analysis.

Credit reference to aspects of the following:

- nationalism – Palestine/Israel
- neighbouring tension – Ukraine/Russia
- lack of development in Africa – poverty/poor health/poor education
- terrorism and religious extremism – Al Qaeda, ISIS.

Any other valid point that meets the criteria described in the general marking instructions.

17 Candidates can be credited in a number of ways **up to a maximum of 6 marks**.

Possible approaches to answering the question:

- NATO and the EU have used both diplomacy and sanctions against Russia to persuade it not to support rebels in the Ukraine but with no success.

  1 mark – accurate but undeveloped point.

- The UN has failed to end the ongoing conflict between Israel and Palestine. The Israeli Government has ignored the UN resolution to build no more settlements and Hamas continues to attack Israeli citizens.

  2 marks – accurate point with development.

- UN action to support the new country of South Sudan has failed to ensure a peaceful and prosperous future. Despite providing economic aid to the new government to ensure political stability, a civil war broke out. This has been a disaster for its citizens. Since December 2013, more than a million people have fled the country, schools have closed and massive food shortages now exist. Many have fled the country to become refugees in neighbouring states. The UN has organised peace talks and hopes that the ceasefire will last.

  4 marks – accurate point with development, exemplification and analysis.

Credit reference to aspects of the following:

- Child soldiers – War Child has had success in the DRC in rehabilitating and reintegrating children involved in conflict back into normal life. But it's a failure because much of the DRC is still in conflict and turmoil.
- Syria – the UN has been successful in feeding and housing refugees in neighbouring countries but has been a failure in being unable to agree collective action due to the Russian veto.
- Libya – the military power of NATO successfully deposed the dictatorship of Colonel Gaddafi but it has failed to make more progress in the country due to tribal/religious conflict.

Any other valid point that meets the criteria described in the general marking instructions.

18 Candidates can be credited in a number of ways **up to a maximum of 8 marks**.

Possible approaches to answering the question:

The progress made in reducing deaths from malaria

Conclusion

Significant progress has been made in reducing deaths from malaria.

1 mark – valid conclusion.

Evidence

The number of deaths since 2000 has been almost halved. In 2000, over 800,000 people died from malaria. In 2015, it was 450,000. Swaziland could soon become the first country in sub-saharan Africa to eradicate the disease (Sources 1 and 3).

2 marks – conclusion with evidence from two sources.

The progress among rich countries to achieve the agreed GNI target on development spending

Conclusion

Progress has been very poor with only one country achieving the agreed target.

1 mark – valid conclusion.

Evidence

Only the UK's contribution of 0.7% of GDI has reached the target, with the USA only contributing 0.2% of its GDP. Italy has contributed even less than the USA with a miserly figure of 0.16% (Sources 1 and 2).

2 marks – conclusion with evidence from two sources.

The link between regional poverty and the existence of killer diseases

Conclusion

The region with the lowest wealth per adult (Africa) has the highest rate of those suffering from malaria and HIV/AIDS.

1 mark – valid conclusion.

Evidence

Africa has the highest number of those infected by malaria and HIV/AIDS and has by far the lowest regional average wealth per adult – for every 100 world citizens experiencing HIV/AIDS, 75 live in the poorest region, Africa. Even the next highest in regional poverty, South America, is over five times wealthier than the African figure of 5000 dollars (Sources 1 and 2).

2 marks – conclusion with evidence from two sources.

Practice Paper B

Section 1

Part A

1 Candidates can be credited in a number of ways **up to a maximum of 4 marks**.

Possible approaches to answering the question:

- One way that an MSP can represent their constituents in the Scottish Parliament is by asking questions during debates.

  1 mark – accurate but undeveloped point.

- One way that an MSP can represent their constituents in the Scottish Parliament is by asking a Parliamentary question. MSPs can do this during First Minister's Questions and Question Time.

  2 marks – accurate point with development.

- One way that an MSP can represent their constituents in the Scottish Parliament is by asking a Parliamentary question. MSPs can do this during First Minister's Questions and Question Time. They can put forward either a written question or ask one verbally in Parliament. For example, at the time when Tata Steel closed in Motherwell, the local MSP raised this issue in Parliament by asking the First Minister what the Government was doing to find alternative employment for those affected.

  3 marks – accurate point with development and exemplification.

Credit reference to aspects of the following:

- MSPs can ask questions during First Minister's Question Time.
- They can also ask individual Ministers questions in the Scottish Parliament (Question Time).
- They can take part in and start debates about an issue that affect constituents, such as a factory closure or nuclear bases.
- They can introduce a Member's Bill in Parliament.
- They can vote during Decision Time.
- They can also take part in Committees within the Scottish Parliament.

Any other valid point that meets the criteria described in the general marking instructions.

2 Candidates can be credited in a number of ways **up to a maximum of 8 marks**.

Possible approaches to answering the question:

- Some people believe that the voting system used to elect MSPs has many strengths as it is a roughly proportionate voting system.

  1 mark – accurate but undeveloped point.

- Some people believe that the voting system used to elect MSPs has many strengths as it is a roughly proportionate voting system. This means that the percentage of votes cast for a particular party is roughly equal to the percentage of seats that the party wins. For example, if the Lib Dems get 8% of the vote they will around 8% of the total number of seats.

  2 marks – accurate points but undeveloped

- Some people believe that the voting system used to elect MSPs has many strengths. One of the strengths is that it is a Proportional Representation (PR) system which means that it will be fairer for representation as it is roughly proportionate and the percentage of votes cast for a party will equal the percentage of seats won. In 2011, the Conservative party won 13% of the votes and ended up with 12% of MSPs. This is a fair system of voting and makes sure that each vote for a party is worth the same as a vote for any other party.

3 marks – accurate point with development and exemplification.

Credit reference to aspects of the following:

- The Additional Member System (AMS) is a broadly proportionate voting system which means that the percentage of votes cast for a party roughly equals the number of seats won. Therefore, it can be seen as being fairer and better reflects the views of the voters.
- AMS allows for smaller parties such as the Greens to be better represented in Parliament, therefore allowing more opinions and views to be heard in the Parliament.
- AMS is more likely to lead to fewer wasted votes as all votes should have an equal value and should encourage greater participation.
- AMS is more likely to lead to coalition government with more parties involved in the decision-making process. This is more likely to lead to compromise and more voters' views and opinions being heard.

Any other valid point that meets the criteria described in the general marking instructions.

3 Candidates can be credited in a number of ways **up to a maximum of 8 marks.**

Possible approaches to answering the question:

Evidence to support the view of Bruce Hart:

- One reason to support the view of Bruce Hart is that Source 1 states the 'No' campaign won the referendum.

  1 mark – accurate use of Source 1 but minimal development.

- One reason to support the view of Bruce Hart can be found in Source 1. Source 1 shows that the 'No' campaign won. This is supported by evidence from Source 1 which shows that 'No' won with over 55% of the vote compared to the 'Yes' campaign's 45%.

  2 marks – accurate use of information from Source 1.

- One reason to support the view of Bruce Hart can be found in Source 1. Source 1 states that the counting of votes was done by council areas. There are 32 council areas in Scotland. Source 2 shows that out of these 32 areas, the 'No' campaign won 28 out of 32 showing that this was a clear victory for 'No' and a major disappointment for 'Yes'.

  3 marks – accurate use of information from two sources with evaluative comment.

Reference to aspects of the following will be credited:

- The 'No' campaign won by 55% to 45%.
- 28 out of 32 council areas voted for the 'No' campaign compared to just 4 for 'Yes'.
- In areas such as Orkney and East Renfrewshire, more than 60% of voters voted 'No'.
- Around 60% of voters in Edinburgh and Aberdeen voted 'No'.

Evidence to oppose the view of Bruce Hart:

- One reason to oppose the view of Bruce Hart can be found in Source 2. It states that Scotland's biggest city, Glasgow, voted 'Yes' in the referendum. This shows that it can't be all bad for 'Yes' if they managed to convince the majority of voters in a city the size of Glasgow.

  2 marks – accurate use of Source 2 with evaluate comment.

- One reason to oppose the view of Bruce Hart can be found in Source 2. It states that Scotland's biggest city, Glasgow, voted 'Yes' in the referendum. This is backed up by evidence from Source 3 which shows that almost 54% of Glasgow voters voted 'Yes' in the referendum.

  2 marks – accurate use of information from Sources 2 and 3.

- One reason to oppose the view of Bruce Hart can be found in Source 2. It states that Scotland's biggest city, Glasgow, voted 'Yes' in the referendum. This is backed up by evidence from Source 3 which shows that almost 54% of Glasgow voters voted 'Yes' in the referendum. This shows that it can't be all bad for 'Yes' if they managed to convince the majority of voters in a city the size of Glasgow.

2 marks – accurate use of information from Sources 1 and 2 with evaluative comment.

Reference to aspects of the following will be credited:

- Over 1.6 million voters voted 'Yes'.
- The winning margin for 'No' was not as big as had been predicted earlier.
- The 'Yes' campaign engaged with many young new voters.
- The majority of voters under 55 years voted for 'Yes'.
- 'Yes' won in Glasgow and Dundee.

Part B

4 Candidates can be credited in a number of ways **up to a maximum of 4 marks**.

Possible approaches to answering the question:

- One way that an MP can represent their constituents in the UK Parliament is by asking questions during debates.

  1 mark – accurate but undeveloped point.

- One way that an MP can represent their constituents in the UK Parliament is by asking a Parliamentary question. MPs can do this during Prime Minister's Questions and Question Time.

  2 marks – accurate point with development.

- One way that an MP can represent their constituents in the UK Parliament is by asking a Parliamentary question. MPs can do this during Prime Minister's Questions and Question Time. They can put forward either a written question or ask one verbally in Parliament. For example, during flooding in Cumbria, the local MP raised this issue in Parliament by asking the Environment Minister what the Government was doing to help his constituents and to prevent further flooding.

  3 marks – accurate point with development and exemplification.

Credit reference to aspects of the following:

- MPs can ask questions during Prime Minister's Question Time.
- They can also ask individual Ministers questions in the UK Parliament
- They can take part in and start debates about an issue that affects constituents, such as a factory closure.
- They can introduce a Private Member's Bill in the UK Parliament.
- They can vote on legislation and participate during debates.

Any other valid point that meets the criteria described in the general marking instructions.

5 Candidates can be credited in a number of ways **up to a maximum of 8 marks**.

Possible approaches to answering the question:

- First Past The Post (FPTP) can be seen to have many strengths as it allows for the voter to have a strong link between themselves and their elected representatives.

  1 mark – accurate but undeveloped point.

- One reason that FPTP can be seen to have many strengths is because it is more likely to lead to one party winning the election and forming the Government. This is a strength as it means that a party can focus on running the country rather than doing deals and compromising with other parties.

  2 marks – accurate points but undeveloped.

- One reason that FPTP can be seen to have many strengths is because it is more likely to lead to one party winning the election and forming the Government. This is a strength as it means that a party can focus on running the country rather than doing deals and compromising with other parties. For example, the 2015 General Election saw the Conservatives and David Cameron become the Government and Prime Minister. They won a clear majority and are now able to govern without having to rely on other parties.

  3 marks – accurate point with development and exemplification.

Credit reference to aspects of the following:

- FPTP is a tried and tested voting system that has been used for many years. It is widely understood by voters and easy to use. It usually leads to a quick and decisive result.
- It can be seen to be fair as it allows the candidates with the largest number of votes in a constituency to win the seat.

- It usually leads to a clear winner nationally with one party forming the Government without the need for compromise and coalitions.
- FPTP provides for a strong link between individual MPs and the voters they represent.

Any other valid point that meets the criteria described in the general marking instructions.

6 Candidates can be credited in a number of ways **up to a maximum of 8 marks**.

Possible approaches to answering the question:

Evidence to support the view of David Trotter:

- One reason to support the view of David Trotter is that Source 1 states that Labour went from being the largest party in Scotland to having just one MP.

  1 mark – evidence drawn from Source 1.

- One reason to support the view of David Trotter is that Source 1 states that Labour went from being the largest party in Scotland to having just one MP. Source 1 also shows that the leader of the Labour Party resigned just after the election.

  2 marks – accurate use of evidence from different parts of Source 1.

- David Trotter is correct as Source 2 states that Labour's grip on Scotland has gone. This can be backed up by evidence from Source 1 which states that Labour used to be the largest party in Scotland, however this changed when they lost all but one seat north of the border. By losing so many seats, this indicates that David Trotter is correct.

  3 marks – accurate us of use of evidence drawn from two sources with evaluative terminology.

Reference to aspects of the following will be credited:

- Conservative Party became the largest party in Parliament.
- Ed Miliband resigned immediately after the election.
- Labour lost in four of the six age groups.
- Labour lost control of Scotland. SNP became the largest party.

Evidence to oppose the view of David Trotter:

- One reason to oppose the view of David Trotter can be found in Source 2. This states that when the election statistics are broken down, things aren't as bad as they appear with Labour's share of the vote increasing. Clearly, if Labour's vote went up then this isn't a major disaster for them.

  2 marks – accurate use of Source 2 with evaluate comment.

- One reason to oppose the view of David Trotter can be found in Source 2. This states that when the election statistics are broken down, things aren't as bad as they appear with Labour's share of the vote increasing. This is backed up with evidence from Source 3 which shows that Labour's share of the vote increased by 1.5%. Clearly, if Labour's share of the vote went up then this isn't a major disaster for them.

  3 marks – accurate use of evidence drawn from two sources with evaluative comment.

Reference to aspects of the following will be credited:

- Increase in Labour's share of the vote.
- More voters aged 18–24 voted Labour than voted Conservative.
- More voters aged 25–34 voted Labour than voted Conservative.

Section 2

Part C

7 Candidates can be credited in a number of ways **up to a maximum of 6 marks**.

Possible approaches to answering the question:

- One way that Government has tried to tackle social inequality is by introducing the Equality Act.

  1 mark – accurate but undeveloped point.

- One way that Government has tried to tackle social inequality is by introducing the Equality Act. This protects people from being discriminated against for their gender, age and other characteristics.

  2 marks – accurate point with development.

- One way that Government has tried to tackle social inequality is by introducing the Equality Act. This protects people from being discriminated against for their gender, age and other characteristics. It makes sure than men and women get paid the same for doing work of equal value, such as a school janitor and school cleaner.

  3 marks – accurate point with development and exemplification.

Credit reference to aspects of the following:

Government policies such as:

- various benefits: Universal Credit, Job Seeker's Allowance
- National Minimum Wage/National Living Wage
- free prescriptions and eye tests in Scotland
- Equality Act and Equality and Human Rights Commission (EHRC)
- National Health Service
- health promotions and campaigns.

Candidates can make reference to social inequalities such as health inequalities, wealth inequalities/poverty and inequalities between groups such as gender, race, etc.

Any other valid point that meets the criteria described in the general marking instructions.

8 Candidates can be credited in a number of ways **up to a maximum of 6 marks**.

Possible approaches to answering the question:

- One reason why some groups are more likely to suffer social inequality than others is because of poverty.

  1 mark – accurate but undeveloped point.

- One reason why some groups are more likely to suffer social inequality than others is because of poverty. People who suffer from poverty are more likely to suffer inequalities such as poor health.

  2 marks – accurate point with development.

- One reason why some groups are more likely to suffer social inequality than others is because of poverty. People who suffer from poverty are more likely to suffer inequalities from illnesses such as diabetes, strokes and lower life expectancy. Poverty also means that they are socially excluded from activities such as holidays.

  3 marks – accurate point with development and exemplification.

Credit reference to aspects of the following:

Candidates can discuss reasons why groups suffer inequalities. This can include:

- influence of poverty on specific groups such as children, families, lone parent families, etc.
- unemployment
- those suffering poverty more likely to suffer poorer health
- gender – women are more likely to do poorer paid jobs, 5Cs (caring, cashiering, catering, cleaning and clinical occupations), part time work, the 'glass ceiling', discrimination.

Any other valid point that meets the criteria described in the general marking instructions.

9 Candidates can be credited in a number of ways **up to a maximum of 8 marks**.

Possible approaches to answering the question:

Benefits issues and referrals to foodbanks:

Conclusion

Benefits issues are often the cause of many referrals to foodbanks.

1 mark – valid conclusion.

Evidence

Source 1 states that 'benefits issues such as benefit changes and delays to payments are often the reasons that many individuals are referred to foodbanks'. This is backed up by evidence from Source 2 that shows that delays and changes account for over 40% of foodbank referrals.

2 marks – conclusion with evidence from two sources.

Benefit sanctions and the use of foodbanks since 2010

Conclusion

Benefit sanctions have led to many people using foodbanks.

1 mark – valid conclusion.

Evidence

Source 1 states that benefit sanctions have led to many individuals turning to foodbanks. This is backed up by evidence from Source 3 which shows that foodbank use has increased from 61,488 in 2010 to over 1 million in 2014.

2 marks – conclusion with evidence from one source.

Foodbanks and the services provided by them

Conclusion

Foodbanks offer users a mix of services to meet their needs.

1 mark – valid conclusion.

Evidence

Source 1 states that foodbanks offer a mix of services. This is backed up by evidence from Source 2 which shows that they not only provide food parcels. Many of them also provide hot food.

2 marks – conclusion with evidence from two sources.

Part D

10 Candidates can be credited in a number of ways **up to a maximum of 6 marks**.

Possible approaches to answering the question:

- Apart from prison, courts can use different sentences such as community payback orders.

  1 mark – accurate but undeveloped point.

- Apart from prison, courts can use different sentences such as community payback orders. Community payback orders require offenders to carry out work in their local area such as clearing rivers or mending fences.

  2 marks – accurate point with development.

- Courts can sentence an offender to drug treatment and testing orders. These sentences require the offender to go through a programme to help with their addictions. They have to remain off drugs or alcohol while they are taking part in these programmes.

  3 marks – accurate point with development and exemplification.

Credit reference to aspects of the following:

- fines
- community payback orders
- probation orders
- restriction of liberty orders (tagging)
- supervised attendance orders
- children's hearing system
- restorative justice programmes.

Any other valid point that meets the criteria described in the general marking instructions.

11 Candidates can be credited in a number of ways **up to a maximum of 6 marks**.

Possible approaches to answering the question:

- One reason why some groups are more likely to be victims of crime is due to age.

  1 mark – accurate but undeveloped point.

- One reason why some groups are more likely to be victims of crime is due to their age. Young people are more likely to be victims of crimes such as mugging and assault.

  2 marks – accurate point with development.

- One reason why some groups are more likely to be victims of crime is due to their age. Young people and the elderly are more likely to be victims of crime than other groups. Young people stand a greater chance of being mugged or assaulted than other groups whereas elderly people are more likely to be the target of burglary due to being seen as vulnerable.

  3 marks – accurate point with development and exemplification.

Credit reference to aspects of the following:

- Age – young people are more likely to be victims of crime than any other group in society. The elderly are also likely to be targeted.
- Gender – males are more likely to be victims of violent crimes such as assault.
- Gender – females are more likely to be victims of sexual crime.
- Young households and the unemployed are both more than twice as likely to be the victims of violence as the average person. Lone parents and private renters are also at high risk.
- Young households, lone parents and the unemployed are all more than twice as likely to be burgled compared to the average household.
- The poor are twice as likely to be victims of crime than other income groups.

Any other valid point that meets the criteria described in the general marking instructions.

12 Candidates can be credited in a number of ways **up to a maximum of 8 marks**.

Possible approaches to answering the question:

Overall clear up rate compared to clear up rate for specific crimes

Conclusion

The overall clear up rate has increased but some crimes have shown a decrease.

1 mark – valid conclusion.

Evidence

Source 1 states that the overall clear up rate has increased, however Source 3 shows that for some crimes such as dishonesty, the clear up rate has decreased from 37% to 36%.

2 marks – conclusion with evidence from two sources.

Crime rates and geographical location

Conclusion

There are geographical differences in the number of crimes committed.

1 mark – valid conclusion.

Evidence

Source 1 states that there is a difference in crime rates between the most and least populated areas. This is backed up by evidence from Source 3 which shows that the highest crime figures are for cities such as Glasgow and Edinburgh compared to the lowest areas such as Orkney and Shetland.

2 marks – conclusion with evidence from one source.

Overall crime rate compared to individual crime rates

Conclusion

Overall, crime is falling but some crimes are continuing to rise.

1 mark – valid conclusion.

Evidence

Source 1 states that there is a steadily decreasing crime rate in Scotland. However, this is not the case for all crimes. For example, sexual crime has increased by 11%.

2 marks – conclusion with evidence from two sources.

Section 3

Part E

13 Candidates can be credited in a number of ways **up to a maximum of 4 marks**.

Possible approaches to answering the question:

South Africa

- One way that people can participate is by voting in elections.

  1 mark – accurate but undeveloped point.

- One way that people can participate is by joining a political party such as the African National Congress. Once they have joined a party they can take part in creating policies and campaigning for the party.

  2 marks – accurate point with development.

- One way that people can participate is by joining a political party such as the African National Congress. Once they have joined a party they can take part in creating policies and campaigning for the party. They can also stand for a position within the party either at a local or national level or even as an election candidate to represent their political party and to fight for their policies.

  4 marks – accurate point with development, exemplification and analysis.

The USA

- One way that people can participate is by voting in elections.

  1 mark – accurate but undeveloped point.

- One way that people can participate is by joining a political party such as the Democratic Party. Once they have joined a party they can take part in creating policies and campaigning for the party.

  2 marks – accurate point with development.

- One way that people can participate is by joining a political party such as the Republican Party. Once they have joined a party they can take part in creating policies and campaigning for the party. They can also stand for a position within the party either at a local or national level or even as an election candidate to represent their political party and to fight for their policies.

  4 marks – accurate point with development, exemplification and analysis.

Credit reference to aspects of the following:

- Voting in elections.
- Joining a party and being active within it.
- Standing as an electoral candidate, helping candidates during elections.
- Campaigning on issues either as an individual or as part of a group.

Any other valid point that meets the criteria described in the general marking instructions.

14 Candidates can be credited in a number of ways **up to a maximum of 6 marks**.

Possible approaches to answering the question:

The USA

- In the USA health inequalities still exist despite the introduction of the Affordable Care Act.

  1 mark – accurate but undeveloped point.

- The USA does not have a state-funded National Health Service which we have in the UK. Health provision is provided mostly through private health insurance companies. Many people cannot afford the payments and cannot always get the treatment they deserve.

  2 marks – accurate point with development.

- In the USA health inequalities continue to exist. One reason is that people have to buy private medical insurance. This means that many poor people, despite help from Obama's reforms, have only limited or no health insurance. This means that they receive only very basic medical care. This can shorten their lives or prevent them from working. This can impact most on ethnic minorities with one in four Hispanics having no health insurance compared to one in ten whites.

  4 marks – accurate point with development, exemplification and analysis.

China

- In China there are inequalities between rural and urban areas.

  1 mark – accurate but undeveloped point.

- In China there are inequalities between the poor rural communities and the rich urban areas. In the rural areas most people work in low paid agricultural jobs and have a low standard of living. In contrast many urban workers have highly paid employment working for the state or multi-national companies.

  2 marks – accurate point with development.

- In China there are vast inequalities in terms of housing, education and income between the migrant workers who come to the cities for work and those with a residence permit and middle class background. Migrant workers receive low pay and have to live in substandard homes. If they bring their families they will find it difficult to get them into schools. Middle class Chinese people have a high income and live in modern homes. Migrant workers are caught in the poverty trap.

  3 marks – accurate point with development, exemplification and analysis.

Credit reference to aspects of the following:

- educational inequalities
- issues relating to health and healthcare inequalities
- income and employment inequalities
- housing inequalities
- law and order issues.

Any other valid point that meets the criteria described in the general marking instructions.

15 Candidates can be credited in a number of ways **up to a maximum of 10 marks**.

Possible approaches to answering the question:

For Option 1:

- One reason why I have chosen Option 1 is because Hilary believes that the economy is an important issue for voters.

  1 mark – evidence drawn from Source 1.

- One reason why I have chosen Option 1 is because Source 1 shows that the economy is an important issue for voters. This is backed up by evidence from Source 2 which says that she will grow the economy if she is elected. This means that she will meet the needs of the voters.

  3 marks – detailed evidence drawn from two sources with evaluative terminology.

- Hilary is the best option because she believes that the economy is the most important issue for Pimlico. This is from Source 2. This is backed up by evidence from Source 3 which shows that 86% of voters believe the election to be the most important issue.

  2 marks – evidence drawn from Sources 2 and 3.

Against Option 1:

- She said that voters are worried about terrorism but the sources show that only 31% of voters agree that terrorism is an issue.

  2 marks – evaluative terminology with limited evidence.

Reference to aspects of the following will be credited:

- Healthcare as an important issue for voters.
- Jobs and the economy are important.

For Option 2:

- Option 2 would be the best choice as Ben Curtis said in Source 2 that he would focus on tourism in order to grow the economy and create jobs. Source 3 shows that tourism is an important issue for voters.

  2 marks – evidence drawn from Sources 2 and 3.

- Option 2 would be the best choice as Ben Curtis said in Source 2 that he would focus on tourism in order to grow the economy and create jobs. Source 3 shows that tourism is an important issue for voters. This means that Option 2 is the best candidate to meet and match the needs of the voters.

  3 marks – detailed evidence drawn from two sources with evaluative terminology.

Against Option 2:

- He would be tough on immigration. However, voters don't rate this issue highly.

  2 marks – evaluative terminology with limited evidence.

Reference to aspects of the following will be credited:

- Economic issues are important to voters.
- Law and order priorities and issues.

Any other valid point that meets the criteria described in the general marking instructions.

Part F

16 Candidates can be credited in a number of ways **up to a maximum of 4 marks**.

Possible approaches to answering the question:

- International conflicts such as terrorism can cause high numbers of refugees in individual nations.

  1 mark – accurate but undeveloped point.

- International conflicts such as terrorism can cause high numbers of refugees in individual nations. The increase of terrorism in Syria has seen a huge increase of refugees in countries such as Turkey as well as in European nations such as Germany.

  2 marks – accurate point with development.

- International conflicts such as terrorism can cause high numbers of refugees in individual nations. The increase of terrorism in Syria has seen a huge increase of refugees in countries such as Turkey as well as in European nations such as Germany. This has led to huge pressure being put on the countries' economies and has also led to tensions within these countries. This shows that international issues can have a big impact on individual countries.

  4 marks – accurate point with development, exemplification and analysis.

Credit reference to aspects of the following:

- Terrorism – the impact on individual countries, e.g. Iraq, Afghanistan, Syria. Displacement, refugees, economic impact, health impact. Increased insecurity.
- HIV/AIDS – impact on populations of specific countries – economic development, impact on health.
- Development – impact on specific nations, lack of economic growth, increased poverty.

Any other valid point that meets the criteria described in the general marking instructions.

17 Candidates can be credited in a number of ways **up to a maximum of 6 marks**.

Possible approaches to answering the question:

- Some people believe that organisations such as the UN have had limited success in tackling issues such as poor health in the developing world. This is because despite some improvements poor health still exists.

  1 mark – accurate but undeveloped point.

- NATO sees one of its main roles as defeating international terrorism. It has had some success such as using drones to target ISIS leaders, however attacks such as the two in Paris in 2015 show that terrorism hasn't fully been defeated.

  2 marks – accurate point with development.

- NATO sees one of its main roles as defeating international terrorism. It has had some success such as using drones to target ISIS leaders, however attacks such as the two in Paris in 2015 show that terrorism hasn't fully been defeated. In the last four years the number of terrorist incidents across the world has trebled and parts of the world such as the Middle East have seen a big increase in terrorist attacks.

  4 marks – accurate point with development, exemplification and analysis.

Credit reference to aspects of the following:

- The Democratic Republic of the Congo (DRC) – NATO has had success in parts of the DRC in ending civil war but has been a failure because much of the DRC is still in conflict and turmoil.
- Syria – the UN has been successful in feeding and housing refugees in neighbouring countries but has been a failure in being unable to agree collective action due to the Russian veto.
- Libya – the military power of NATO successfully deposed the dictatorship of Colonel Gaddafi but it has failed to make more progress in the country due to tribal/religious conflict.

Any other valid point that meets the criteria described in the general marking instructions.

18 Candidates can be credited in a number of ways **up to a maximum of 10 marks**.

Possible approaches to answering the question:

For Option 1:

- I would choose Option 1 because this candidate believes that healthcare is a very important issue for the African Union.

  1 mark – evidence drawn from Source 1.

- I would choose Option 1 because this candidate believes that healthcare is a very important issue for the African Union. This is backed up by evidence from Source 3 which shows that healthcare issues are the equal most important issue for the area.

  2 marks – evaluative terminology with limited evidence.

- I would choose Option 1 because this candidate believes that healthcare is a very important issue for the African Union. This is backed up by evidence from Source 3 which shows that healthcare issues are the equal most important issue for the area. This is backed up by evidence in Source 1 that Africa continues to suffer from poor healthcare showing that Option 1 has the best priorities for the area.

  3 marks – detailed evidence drawn from two sources with evaluative terminology.

Against Option 1:

- The candidate says that HIV/AIDS is a top issue but polls say otherwise.

  2 marks – evaluative terminology with limited evidence.

Reference to aspects of the following will be credited:

- Healthcare, HIV/AIDS and drug prices.

For Option 2:

- I have chosen Option 2 because according to Source 1 only 9 out of 54 member states are democracies. Option 2 would look to increase democracy across Africa.

  2 marks – evidence drawn from Sources 1 and 2.

- I have chosen Option 2 because according to Source 1 only 9 out of 54 member states are democracies. Option 2 would look to increase democracy across Africa. This shows that candidate 2 is the best candidate as they are trying to meet the needs of Africa.

  3 marks – detailed evidence drawn from two sources with evaluative terminology.

Against Option 2:

- The candidate says that terrorism is a big issue but statistics say otherwise.

  2 marks – evaluative terminology with limited evidence.

Reference to aspects of the following will be credited:

- Experience of working with African Union.
- Promotion of greater democracy.

Practice Paper C

Section 1

Part A

1 Candidates can be credited in a number of ways **up to a maximum of 6 marks**.

Possible approaches to answering the question:

- One way that people can participate during elections is by campaigning for a particular party.

  1 mark – accurate but undeveloped point.

- One way that people can participate during an election is by campaigning for a party such as Scottish Labour or the SNP. Campaigning could mean giving out leaflets in the street about your chosen party's policies.

  2 marks – accurate point with development.

- One way that people can participate during elections is by canvassing voters. Canvassing means contacting voters and asking them who they intend to vote for. Canvassers try to convince voters why they should vote for their chosen candidate or party such as the Scottish Greens or Scottish Tories.

  3 marks – accurate point with development and exemplification.

Credit reference to aspects of the following:

- Join a political party and help campaign for them.
- Canvass voters.
- Publicise their chosen party by putting up posters.
- Help to organise public meetings.
- Provide transport to allow elderly voters to get to the polling station.

Any other valid point that meets the criteria described in the general marking instructions.

2 Candidates can be credited in a number of ways **up to a maximum of 6 marks**.

Possible approaches to answering the question:

- People should use their vote in Scotland as it is our democratic right that many other people around the world don't have.

  1 mark – accurate but undeveloped point.

- People should use their vote in Scotland as it means that your voice is being heard in the Scottish Parliament. If you don't vote, then you don't have the right to criticise the Scottish Government.

  2 marks – accurate point with development.

- People should use their vote in Scotland because many people have fought and given up their lives in order for us to have rights and freedoms, such as the right to vote and if we don't vote then we are disrespecting the sacrifice that many Scottish people have made fighting for our right to vote.

  3 marks – accurate point with development and exemplification.

Credit reference to aspects of the following:

- Voting is a democratic right in Scotland. Many countries around the world don't have the same rights as us. We should exercise our rights as often as we can.
- If you don't vote, then some people think that you give up the right to criticise the work of the Government.

- People pay tax. By voting, you can have a bigger say in how that tax is spent.
- By not voting, voters could be allowing extremist parties the opportunity to gain some power.
- It is important to vote in order to get a government that represents the majority of the population. If turnout is low, parties are elected with very small percentages of voters voting for them.

Any other valid point that meets the criteria described in the general marking instructions.

3 Candidates can be credited in a number of ways **up to a maximum of 8 marks**.

Possible approaches to answering the question:

Age and voter turnout

Conclusion

A person's age can influence whether they turn out or not.

1 mark – valid conclusion.

Evidence

Source 1 states that there are clear differences between the turnout of young and old voters. This is backed up by evidence from Source 3 which shows that voters over the age of 55 were more likely to vote than those aged between 16 and 34. 92% of older voters voted in the independence referendum compared to 72% of younger voters.

2 marks – conclusion with evidence from two sources.

Social group and voter turnout

Conclusion

A person's social group or class can influence whether they turn out or not.

1 mark – valid conclusion.

Evidence

Source 1 states that the more prosperous or wealthy you are, the more likely you are to vote in elections compared to poorer voters. This is backed up by evidence in Source 2 which shows that wealthier voters in groups ABC1 are more likely to vote than those in poorer social groups C2DE. 88% of better off voters voted in the independence referendum compared to 79% of poorer voters.

2 marks – conclusion with evidence from two sources.

Type of election and voter turnout

Conclusion

Turnout varies depending on the type of election.

1 mark – valid conclusion.

Evidence

Source 1 states that some elections are more likely to have a higher turnout than others. This is backed up in Source 2 which shows that turnout ranges from 33% for a European election compared to 84% for the Independence Referendum.

2 marks – conclusion with evidence from two sources.

Part B

4   Candidates can be credited in a number of ways **up to a maximum of 6 marks**.

Possible approaches to answering the question:

- One way that people can participate during elections is by campaigning for a particular party.

   1 mark – accurate but undeveloped point.

- One way that people can participate during a General Election is by campaigning for a party such as Labour or the Conservatives. Campaigning could mean giving out leaflets in the street about your chosen party's policies.

   2 marks – accurate point with development.

- One way that people can participate during General Elections is by canvassing voters. Canvassing means contacting voters and asking them who they intend to vote for. Canvassers try to convince voters why they should vote for their chosen candidate or party such as the Greens or Tories.

   3 marks – accurate point with development and exemplification.

Credit reference to aspects of the following:

- Join a political party and help campaign for them.
- Canvass voters.
- Publicise their chosen party by putting up posters.
- Help to organise public meetings.
- Provide transport to allow elderly voters to get to the polling station.

Any other valid point that meets the criteria described in the general marking instructions.

5   Candidates can be credited in a number of ways **up to a maximum of 6 marks**.

Possible approaches to answering the question:

- People should use their vote in the UK as it is our democratic right that many other people around the world don't have.

   1 mark – accurate but undeveloped point.

- People should use their vote in the UK as it means that your voice is being heard in the UK Parliament. If you don't vote, then you don't have the right to criticise the UK Government.

   2 marks – accurate point with development.

- People should use their vote in the UK because many people have fought and given up their lives in order for us to have rights and freedoms, such as the right to vote and if we don't vote then we are disrespecting the sacrifice that many British people have made fighting for our right to vote.

   3 marks – accurate point with development and exemplification.

Credit reference to aspects of the following:

- Voting is a democratic right in the UK. Many countries around the world don't have the same rights as us. We should exercise our rights as often as we can.
- If you don't vote, then some people think that you give up the right to criticise the work of the Government.
- People pay tax. By voting, you can have a bigger say in how that tax is spent.
- By not voting, voters could be allowing extremist parties the opportunity to gain some power.
- It is important to vote in order to get a government that represents the majority of the population. If turnout is low, parties are elected with very small percentages of voters voting for them.

Any other valid point that meets the criteria described in the general marking instructions.

6 Candidates can be credited in a number of ways **up to a maximum of 8 marks**.

Possible approaches to answering the question:

Age and voter turnout

Conclusion

A person's age can influence whether they turn out or not.

1 mark – valid conclusion.

Evidence

Source 1 states that there are clear differences between the turnout of young and old voters. This is backed up by evidence from Source 3 which shows that voters over the age of 55 were more likely to vote than those aged between 16 and 34. 77% of older voters voted in the General Election compared to 49% of younger voters.

2 marks – conclusion with evidence from two sources.

Social group and voter turnout

Conclusion

A person's social group or class can influence whether they turn out or not.

1 mark – valid conclusion.

Evidence

Source 1 states that the more prosperous or wealthy you are, the more likely you are to vote in elections compared to poorer voters. This is backed up by evidence in Source 2 which shows that wealthier voters in groups ABC1 are more likely to vote than those in poorer social groups C2DE. 72% of better off voters voted in the General Election compared to 59% of poorer voters.

2 marks – conclusion with evidence from two sources.

Type of election and voter turnout

Conclusion

Turnout varies depending on the type of election.

1 mark – valid conclusion.

Evidence

Source 1 states that some elections are more likely to have a higher turnout than others. This is backed up in Source 2 which shows that turnout ranges from 31% for a council election compared to 67% for the General Election.

2 marks – conclusion with evidence from two sources.

Section 2

Part C

7 Candidates can be credited in a number of ways **up to a maximum of 4 marks**.

Possible approaches to answering the question:

- Social inequality exists in the UK as some people are more likely to have better health than others.

  1 mark – accurate but undeveloped point.

- One way that social inequality exists is when you compare the life expectancy of those in different social classes. Those that are better off in social groups AB are more likely to live longer than those in poorer social groups DE.

  2 marks – accurate point with development.

- Social inequality exists in the UK. One area where it exists is in the area of education. Pupils from poorer backgrounds are less likely to do well at school than those from better off backgrounds. This has an effect on university intake. For example, in some Scottish universities, such as St Andrew's or Edinburgh, there are low numbers of working class students with less than 20% of students at these universities coming from poorer backgrounds.

  4 marks – accurate point with development and exemplification.

Credit reference to aspects of the following:

- evidence of health inequalities
- evidence of housing inequality (homelessness, etc.)
- evidence of educational inequalities (pass marks, achievement rates)
- evidence of child poverty, pensioner poverty
- evidence of gender inequality
- evidence of race/ethnic inequality.

Any other valid point that meets the criteria described in the general marking instructions.

8 Candidates can be credited in a number of ways **up to a maximum of 6 marks**.

Possible approaches to answering the question:

- Some people think that Government policies to tackle a social inequality such as health have been successful as people are now living longer.

  1 mark – accurate but undeveloped point.

- Government policies have had success in tackling gender inequalities. Since the 1980s, the gap between men and women's wages has narrowed to around 15%. Policies such as the National Minimum Wage have had some success.

  2 marks – accurate point with development.

- Inequality still exists in the UK. There have been improvements in health statistics with people now living longer than they did before. However, inequalities still exist as those in higher social groups such as AB are more likely to have less illness and live longer than those who suffer poverty and are in social groups DE.

  3 marks – accurate point with development and exemplification.

Credit reference to aspects of the following:

- Candidates should discuss areas where there have been improvements such as longer life expectancy and better health statistics.

- More women breaking through the 'glass ceiling' in areas such as law and business.
- The Equality Act has led to a narrowing of the gender pay gap and success also in terms of work of equal value pay outs.

Any other valid point that meets the criteria described in the general marking instructions.

9 Candidates can be credited in a number of ways **up to a maximum of 10 marks**.

Possible approaches to answering the question:

For Option 1:

- One reason why I have chosen Option 1 can be found in Source 1. It states people who drink alcohol at an earlier age are more likely to develop alcohol-related problems in later life.

  1 mark – evidence drawn from Source 1 but minimal development.

- One reason why I have chosen Option 1 can be found in Source 1. It states people who drink alcohol at an earlier age are more likely to develop alcohol-related problems in later life. This is backed up by evidence in Source 2 which states that introducing this change would improve the health of young people and decrease their chance of alcohol-related problems over the course of their life.

  2 marks – evaluative terminology with limited evidence.

- Alcohol abuse in Scotland is a problem. Source 1 shows that around 20% of Scots drink more than the recommended amount. This is backed up by evidence from Source 2 which shows a doubling of deaths relating to alcohol since the 1990s. The Scottish people want the Government to do more to tackle this problem (Source 3). This policy would make it harder for young people to buy alcohol and it will improve their health chances.

  3 marks – detailed evidence drawn from three sources with evaluative terminology.

Reference to aspects of the following will be credited:

- Studies have shown that starting drinking at an earlier age can cause more problems in later life (Sources 1 and 2).
- 20% of scots regularly drink to excess (Source 1).
- Doubling of alcohol-related deaths (Source 2).
- Scottish people want the Government to do more to tackle alcohol abuse (Source 3).

Against Option 1:

- See For Option 2 below.

For Option 2:

- One reason why we should keep things as they are can be found in Source 1. This shows that young people are now drinking less than they used to. Their behaviour is changing. There is no need to change the law.

  1 mark – evidence drawn from Source 1.

- There is no need to change the law. Young people aren't the problem. Older people are likely to suffer problems. This group accounts for the highest number of deaths due to alcohol. This is backed up by Source 2 which states that it targets the wrong groups and that more action should be taken to tackle alcohol abuse in older people not the young.

  2 marks – evidence drawn from Sources 1 and 2.

- Yes. The public do want more action (Source 3) but they do not want to see this policy. They would rather see more health promotion campaigns. There is also evidence that the current strategies are working. The message is getting through. Many people are aware of the safe limits and many people stick to and respect these limits (Source 1). There is no need for change.

  3 marks – detailed evidence from two sources with evaluative terminology.

Reference to aspects of the following will be credited:

- The fall in the number of teenage drinkers (Source 1).
- Teenagers will still be able to obtain alcohol. Changing the law won't change that (Source 2).
- Young drinkers are not the main issue. Older drinkers are (Sources 1 and 2).
- The public want the government to do more (Source 3).

Against Option 2:

- See For Option 1 above.

Part D

10 Candidates can be credited in a number of ways **up to a maximum of 4 marks**.

Possible approaches to answering the question:

- One type of crime that wealthier people are more likely to commit is financial crimes such as insider share trading.

  1 mark – accurate but undeveloped point.

- Wealthier people do commit crime. These types of crime tend to be more financial and business related such as VAT fraud or tax evasion where business owners will try to avoid paying the government what they should.

  2 marks – accurate point with development.

- Wealthier people are more likely to commit crime that involves fraud or non-payment of taxes. They are also more likely to commit crimes involving high finance and business. The type of crimes they commit are likely to be linked to their economic status and keeping their position in society.

  3 marks – accurate point with development and exemplification.

Credit reference to aspects of the following:

- types of fraud – VAT fraud, carousel fraud
- tax evasion schemes
- insider share trading
- embezzlement
- insurance fraud
- use of drugs associated with the wealthy, e.g. cocaine use.

Any other valid point that meets the criteria described in the general marking instructions.

11 Candidates can be credited in a number of ways **up to a maximum of 6 marks**.

Possible approaches to answering the question:

- One reason why social deprivation can cause crime is because some poorer people who are socially deprived may turn to crime in order to feed or provide for their families.

  1 mark – accurate but undeveloped point.

- One reason why social deprivation can cause crime is that some people who are socially deprived may also be drug users and they might commit crime in order to pay for and to feed their drug habit.

  2 marks – accurate point with development.

- Social deprivation can cause crime. Some people who are socially deprived may turn to crime in order to have the things that better off people have. They may resort to shoplifting or house breaking to get these things either for themselves or to sell to others in order to get cash for themselves. There is a clear link between growing social deprivation and an increase in crimes such as shoplifting or burglary.

  3 marks – accurate point with development and exemplification.

Credit reference to aspects of the following:

- Some people who suffer social deprivation may commit crime in order to provide for their families. Growing evidence of subsistence theft, mostly from supermarkets.
- Committing crime in order to pay for or feed a substance misuse problem.
- Social deprivation can lead to boredom among groups of young people. Peer pressure and boredom linked to social deprivation can cause increased crime.
- There's a clear correlation between increased social deprivation and specific crimes such as theft and house breaking.

- Social deprivation can put pressure on families and can lead to increased incidence of domestic violence and abuse.

Any other valid point that meets the criteria described in the general marking instructions.

12 Candidates can be credited in a number of ways **up to a maximum of 10 marks**.

Possible approaches to answering the question:

For Option 1:

- We need to change the law and raise the age. Source 1 shows that 66% of young offenders were drunk at the time of their offence.

  1 mark – evidence drawn from Source 1 but minimal development.

- We need to change the law and raise the age. Source 1 shows that 66% of young offenders were drunk at the time of their offence. The facts speak for themselves. The public want the government to do more. By introducing this change, we will cut down on the number of drunk young people and this will lead to a fall in crime.

  2 marks – evaluative terminology with limited evidence.

- We need to change the law. Source 1 shows that alcohol and young people don't mix. It causes crime. It causes violent crime and the cost is too high. We need to tackle this problem. Source 2 shows that it will make our streets safer for people to walk down and it will make our cities safer too.

  3 marks – detailed evidence drawn from two sources with evaluative terminology.

Reference to aspects of the following will be credited:

- Evidence from Source 1 which shows the cost and impact of alcohol, crime and young people.
- Incidence of violence around pubs (Source 1).
- The number of young people under the influence of alcohol at the time of an offence (Source 1).
- The cost of alcohol-related crime and disorder (Source 1).
- Make cities safer (Source 2).
- Public want government to do more (Source 3).

Against Option 1:

- See For Option 2 below.

For Option 2:

- There is no need to change the law. Source 1 shows that violent crime has fallen. Government policies are working.

  1 mark – evidence drawn from Source 1.

- The public don't want this change. They would rather see more police on the beat and more CCTV before they would want this change (Source 3). Source 2 backs this up by saying that the public are happy with the government's approach to tackling violent crime.

  2 marks – evidence drawn from Sources 2 and 3.

- This policy will do nothing to change young people, alcohol and crime. Under 18s currently can access and buy alcohol right now despite it being illegal. You can see this in the hospital admissions figures (Source1). This is backed up by Source 2 that says that underage drinkers will still be able to buy drink. This law won't change that. If young people want to buy drink, they will buy it.

  3 marks – detailed evidence from two sources with evaluative terminology.

Reference to aspects of the following will be credited:

- The fall in violent crime (Source 1).
- Underage drinking is currently an issue (Source 1).
- Teenagers will still be able to obtain alcohol. Changing the law won't change that (Source 2).
- The public want more CCTV and police on the beat rather than a change in the law (Source 3).

Against Option 2:

- See For Option 1 above.

Section 3

Part E

13 Candidates can be credited in a number of ways **up to a maximum of 6 marks**.

Possible approaches to answering the question:

The USA

- One way that the USA has tried to tackle socio-economic issues is by introducing policies such as Temporary Assistance for Needy Families (TANF).

  1 mark – accurate but undeveloped point.

- One way that the USA has tried to tackle socio-economic issues is by introducing policies such as TANF. This provides short-term temporary assistance to families that may have suffered due to unemployment or increased poverty.

  2 marks – accurate point with development.

- One way that the USA has tried to tackle issues is through policies such as the American Recovery and Reinvestment Act (ARRA). This is sometimes known as Obama's Fiscal Stimulus. The government pumped money into the US economy and built roads, schools and hospitals following the global economic crash. This led to more jobs being created and more money being spent which help the economy and lifted some Americans out of poverty.

  4 marks – accurate point with development, exemplification and analysis.

Credit reference to aspects of the following:

- Temporary Assistance for Needy Families (TANF)
- No Child Left Behind (NCLB)
- American Recovery and Reinvestment Act (ARRA) – Obama's Fiscal Stimulus
- Changes to medical insurance cover – ObamaCare
- Food Stamps
- Affirmative Action.

Any other valid point that meets the criteria described in the general marking instructions.

South Africa

- One way that South Africa has tried to tackle social and economic issues is by introducing policies such as Black Economic Empowerment (BEE).

  1 mark – accurate but underdeveloped point.

- One way that South Africa has tried to tackle social and economic issues is by introducing policies such as Black Economic Empowerment (BEE). This policy tries to ensure that all South Africans have the same opportunities to be prosperous and do well.

  2 marks – accurate point with development.

- One way that South Africa has tried to tackle social and economic issues is by introducing policies such as Black Economic Empowerment (BEE). This policy tries to ensure that all South Africans have the same opportunities to be prosperous and do well. BEE attempts to empower black South Africans to own and manage their own businesses. It also encourages them to gain more skills that make them more employable.

  3 marks – accurate point with development and exemplification.

Credit reference to aspects of the following:

- Black Economic Empowerment
- Accelerate and Shared Growth Initiative
- Expanded Public Works Programme

- National Skills Fund
- programmes and strategies designed to ensure access to clean drinking water, sanitation and electricity
- healthcare initiatives designed to tackle the growth of HIV/AIDS.

Any other valid point that meets the criteria described in the general marking instructions.

14 Candidates can be credited in a number of ways **up to a maximum of 6 marks**.

Possible approaches to answering the question:

The USA

- The USA can claim to have global influence as it is one of the most powerful countries in the world.
  1 mark – accurate but undeveloped point.

- The USA can claim to have global influence as it is seen as being one of the leading countries in organisations such as the United Nations or NATO. It is the largest financial contributor to NATO.
  2 marks – accurate point with development.

- The USA is one of the most powerful countries in the world. It is economically powerful, militarily powerful and has a great deal of political power in organisations such as the UN, NATO, the world bank and the IMF. Many countries are the USA's allies and it can rely on its influence to get what it wants globally.
  4 marks – accurate point with development, exemplification and analysis.

Credit reference to aspects of the following:

- Permanent member of the United Nations.
- Membership of G7 group of countries.
- Biggest contributor to NATO.
- Examples of economic, military, political influence on the global stage.

Any other valid point that meets the criteria described in the general marking instructions.

China

- China can claim to have global influence as it is one of the largest and fastest growing economies in the world.
  1 mark – accurate but undeveloped point.

- China can claim to have global influence as it is one of the largest and fastest growing economies in the world. In terms of GDP, China's economy is the second largest economy in the world and is expected to overtake the USA and become the largest economy by 2020.
  2 marks – accurate point with development.

- China can claim to have global influence as it is a permanent member of the United Nations Security Council. This means that it is one of only five countries in the United Nations that have the power to veto any proposals brought to the United Nations. It has used its veto to block any sanctions during the Syrian conflict.
  3 marks – accurate point with development and exemplification.

Credit reference to aspects of the following:

- China is a member of G8 and G20
- It's a permanent member of UN Security Council with power of veto.
- China has great and growing economic power. It produces a quarter of the world's wealth.
- It's the second largest economy in world.
- It's the largest and most powerful country in East Asia.
- China is a nuclear power and possesses one of the largest armies in the world.

Any other valid point that meets the criteria described in the general marking instructions.

15 Candidates can be credited in a number of ways **up to a maximum of 8 marks**.

Possible approaches to answering the question:

Evidence to support the view of Isabel Porter:

- One reason to support the view of Isabel Porter is that Source 3 shows that voters are happy with the European Union.

  1 mark – accurate use of Source 3 but minimal development.

- One reason to support the view of Isabel Porter is that Source 3 shows that voters are happy with the European Union. Source 3 shows that 60% of voters in Scotland think that the UK should remain part of the EU.

  2 marks – accurate use of evidence from different parts of Source 3.

- One piece of evidence to support Isabel Porter can be found in Source 2. Source 2 clearly shows that the citizens of France, Germany and Poland feel favourable about the EU. Indeed, the number in each of these countries has risen in the last year with 54% of French, 66% of Germans and 72% of Poles favourable towards the EU. This indicates that they are happy with the EU.

  3 marks – accurate use of evidence drawn from Sources 1 and 2 with evaluative comment.

Reference to aspects of the following will be credited:

- There has been a percentage rise in three of the four countries (Source 2).
- Scotland and England both have a majority of voters wanting to remain in the EU (Source 3).

Evidence to oppose the view of Isabel Porter:

- One piece of evidence to oppose Isabel Porter can be found in Source 1. Source 1 shows that there have been riots in Athens in protest at the EU's role in increasing poverty and unemployment. These riots would indicate that some EU citizens aren't happy with the EU.

  1 mark – accurate use of Source 1 with evaluate comment.

- Isabel Porter is wrong in her view. Source 1 shows that Greeks aren't happy and that Italy doesn't feel favourable towards the EU with the figure falling from 58% to 46%.

  2 marks – accurate use of evidence from Sources 1 and 2.

- Isabel Porter is wrong in her view. Source one shows that Greeks aren't happy and that Italy doesn't feel favourable towards the EU with the figure falling from 58% to 46%. If people are rioting in Athens and the majority of Italians don't feel favourable to the EU then this might indicate that they aren't happy with it.

  3 marks – accurate source of evidence from Sources 1 and 2 with evaluative comment.

Reference to aspects of the following will be credited:

- Protests in Athens against increasing poverty (Source 1).
- Statistical fall in the number of Italians feeling favourable towards the EU.

Part F

16 Candidates can be credited in a number of ways **up to a maximum of 6 marks**.

Possible approaches to answering the question:

- One way that conflicts and issues can affect the international community is because the international community will often have to contribute financially to tackle these issues.

  1 mark – accurate but undeveloped point.

- International conflicts and issues often create problems for the international community. Other countries may need to send peacekeepers into areas where conflict exists such as the Middle East.

  2 marks – accurate point with development.

- The growth of conflict in areas such as Syria has led to increased terrorism across the wider international community. This has meant that countries now need to work together and co-operate in order to tackle this issue. This has had a cost – a human cost due to increased casualties but also an economic cost as countries need to improve their own security and also work with other countries.

  4 marks – accurate point with development, exemplification and analysis.

Credit reference to aspects of the following:

- Impact of terrorism on the wider community – human cost, economic cost, etc. Cost to the international community of peacekeeping, promoting democracy.
- The international community has to fund development projects and development goals. This can be very costly.
- HIV/AIDS – cost to international community of long-term retro viral treatment.
- Conflict can lead to displacement and refugees. This can impact on the wider international community in terms of care, resettlement and security.

Any other valid point that meets the criteria described in the general marking instructions.

17 Candidates can be credited in a number of ways **up to a maximum of 6 marks**.

Possible approaches to answering the question:

- One reason why international organisations attempt to resolve issues and conflicts is in order to create a more peaceful and stable world.

  1 mark – accurate but undeveloped point.

- One reason why international organisations attempt to resolve issues and conflicts is in order to make parts of the world more stable and democratic which usually means that there is greater chance of peace and co-operation rather than war and conflict.

  2 marks – accurate point with development.

- International organisations try to tackle issues and conflicts for a number of reasons. They want people to live longer, to be healthy, prosperous and to live in a world without war and violence. If they can promote stability and democracy around the world then this benefits individuals, nations and the wider global community.

  4 marks – accurate point with development, exemplification and analysis.

Credit reference to aspects of the following:

- To promote peace and security.
- To reduce the chance of conflict and war.
- To promote international co-operation and universal human rights.
- To help improve people's health and to increase life expectancy.
- To promote increased democracy and stability.
- To protect civilians from conflicts and issues.
- To promote greater economic co-operation and trade.

Any other valid point that meets the criteria described in the general marking instructions.

18 Candidates can be credited in a number of ways **up to a maximum of 8 marks**.

Possible approaches to answering the question:

Evidence to support the view of Martin Santini:

- One piece of evidence to support Martin Santini is that Source 2 shows that the number of AIDS deaths and HIV infections has fallen.

  1 mark – accurate use of Source 2 but minimal development.

- Source 1 shows that the African Union works to reduce HIV/AIDS in Africa. Source 2 shows that the number of AIDS deaths and HIV infections has fallen.

  2 marks – accurate use of evidence from Sources 1 and 2.

- Source 1 shows that the African Union works to reduce HIV/AIDS in Africa. Source 2 shows that the number of AIDS deaths and HIV infections has fallen. This fall indicates that the African Union has been effective in tackling this world issue.

  3 marks – accurate use of evidence from Sources 1 and 2 with evaluative comment.

Credit reference to aspects of the following:

- Infant mortality has fallen (Source 1) indicating that the UN has been effective in tackling this global issue.
- HIV/AIDS rates have fallen indicating the AU's effectiveness at tackling this world issue.

Evidence to oppose the view of Martin Santini:

- One reason to oppose Martin's view is that there has been an increase in terrorist attacks. In 2012 there were 6,771 terrorist attacks. This has more than doubled in two years which indicates that organisations haven't been effective.

  2 marks – accurate use of Source 2 with evaluative comment.

- One reason to oppose Martin's view is that NATO's aim is to combat terrorism (Source 1). Source 3 shows that terrorism has increased.

  2 marks – accurate use of evidence from Sources 1 and 3.

- One reason to oppose Martin's view is that NATO hasn't been effective in its aim of combatting terrorism. Source 1 shows that it has been working with its member countries. However, Source 3 shows that the number of terrorist attacks has almost doubled. This shows that NATO hasn't been effective and that Martin is wrong.

  3 marks – accurate use of evidence from Sources 1 and 3 with evaluative comment.

Credit reference to aspects of the following:

- European Union is to promote economic progress as well as peace (Source 1).
- Greece and Athens have seen riots and increased poverty. Many blame the EU (Source 2).
- Unemployment in Greece has increased (Source 2).